Workshop on Sentiment and Subjectivity in Text 2006

AA005760

Held in conjunction with COLING/ACL 2006

Sydney, Australia
22 July 2006

ISBN: 978-1-61738-502-5

Printed from e-media with permission by:

Curran Associates, Inc.
57 Morehouse Lane
Red Hook, NY 12571
www.proceedings.com

Some format issues inherent in the e-media version may also appear in this print version.

Printed by Curran Associates, Inc. (2010)

Association for Computational Linguistics
209 N. Eighth Street
Stroudsburg, Pennsylvania 18360

Phone: 1-570-476-8006
Fax: 1-570-476-0860

acl@aclweb.org

Table of Contents

Preface v

Organizers vii

Workshop Program ix

Extracting Opinions, Opinion Holders, and Topics Expressed in Online News Media Text
Soo-Min Kim and Eduard Hovy 1

Toward Opinion Summarization: Linking the Sources
Veselin Stoyanov and Claire Cardie 9

A System for Summarizing and Visualizing Arguments in Subjective Documents: Toward Supporting Decision Making
Atsushi Fujii and Tetsuya Ishikawa 15

User-directed Sentiment Analysis: Visualizing the Affective Content of Documents
Michelle L. Gregory, Nancy Chinchor, Paul Whitney, Richard Carter, Elizabeth Hetzler and Alan Turner 23

Annotating Attribution in the Penn Discourse TreeBank
Rashmi Prasad, Nikhil Dinesh, Alan Lee, Aravind Joshi and Bonnie Webber 31

Searching for Sentences Expressing Opinions by Using Declaratively Subjective Clues
Nobuaki Hiroshima, Setsuo Yamada, Osamu Furuse and Ryoji Kataoka 39

Exploitation in Affect Detection in Open-Ended Improvisational Text
Li Zhang, John A. Barnden, Robert J. Hendley and Alan M. Wallington 47

Towards a Validated Model for Affective Classification of Texts
Michel Généreux and Roger Evans 55

Author Index 63

Preface

This volume contains the papers prepared for and presented at the Workshop on Sentiment and Subjectivity in Text, held on 22 July 2006 in Sydney, Australia, immediately following COLING/ACL 2006.

Sentiment and subjectivity in text constitute a problem that is orthogonal to typical topic detection tasks in text classification. Despite the lack of a precise definition of sentiment or subjectivity, headway has been made in matching human judgments by automatic means. Such systems can prove useful in a variety of contexts. In many applications it is important to distinguish what an author is talking about from his or her subjective stance towards the topic. If the writing is highly subjective, as for example in an editorial text or comment, the text should be treated differently than if it were a mostly objective presentation of facts, as for example in a news article. Information extraction, summarization, and question answering can benefit from an accurate separation of subjective content from objective content. Furthermore, the particular sentiment expressed by an author towards a topic is important for "opinion mining", i.e. the extraction of prevalent opinions about topics or items from a collection of texts. Similarly, in business intelligence it is important to automatically extract positive and negative perceptions about features of a product or service.

Over the past several years, there has been an increasing number of publications focused on the detection and classification of sentiment and subjectivity in text. The purpose of the workshop is to bring together researchers interested in the topic to share and discuss recent work in the area. The quality and diversity of submissions we received confirmed our belief that this area is and will continue to be a fascinating and fruitful one for some time to come.

We wish to thank all of the authors for submitting papers for consideration, and all of the members of the program committee for their careful and prompt attention to the review process. We also wish to thank our invited speakers, Bing Liu, Nicolas Nicolov, and Franco Salvetti.

Michael Gamon and Anthony Aue
June 2006

Organizers

Chairs:

Michael Gamon and Anthony Aue, Microsoft Research

Program Committee:

Shlomo Argamon, Illinois Institute of Technology
Claire Cardie, Cornell University
Graeme Hirst, University of Toronto
Eduard Hovy, USC Information Sciences Institute
Aravind Joshi, University of Pennsylvania
Jussi Karlgren, Swedish Institute of Computer Science
Roy Lipski, Oxford Catalysts
Nicolas Nicolov, Umbria Inc.
Bo Pang, Cornell University
Ana-Maria Popescu, University of Washington
Dragomir Radev, University of Michigan
Maarten de Rijke, University of Amsterdam
Franco Salvetti, Umbria Inc.
Marc Schröder, DFKI
Michael Strube, EML Research
Pero Subasic, Yahoo Inc.
Peter Turney, National Research Council Canada
Özlem Uzuner, Massachusetts Institute of Technology
Casey Whitelaw, University of Sydney
Janyce Wiebe, University of Pittsburgh

Invited Speakers:

Bing Liu, University of Illinois at Chicago
Nicolas Nicolov and Franco Salvetti, Umbria Inc.

Workshop Program

Saturday, 22 July 2006

9:00–9:15	Welcome and Introductions
9:15–10:00	Invited Talk by Bing Liu: Extracting and Summarizing Opinions on the Web
10:00–10:30	*Extracting Opinions, Opinion Holders, and Topics Expressed in Online News Media Text* Soo-Min Kim and Eduard Hovy
10:30–11:00	Coffee Break
11:00–11:30	*Toward Opinion Summarization: Linking the Sources* Veselin Stoyanov and Claire Cardie
11:30–12:00	*A System for Summarizing and Visualizing Arguments in Subjective Documents: Toward Supporting Decision Making* Atsushi Fujii and Tetsuya Ishikawa
12:00–12:30	*User-directed Sentiment Analysis: Visualizing the Affective Content of Documents* Michelle L. Gregory, Nancy Chinchor, Paul Whitney, Richard Carter, Elizabeth Hetzler and Alan Turner
12:30–1:45	Lunch
1:45–2:30	Invited Talk by Nicolas Nicolov and Franco Salvetti: The Good, the Bad, and the Money: How Industry is Capitalizing on Sentiment
2:30–3:00	*Annotating Attribution in the Penn Discourse TreeBank* Rashmi Prasad, Nikhil Dinesh, Alan Lee, Aravind Joshi and Bonnie Webber
3:00–3:30	*Searching for Sentences Expressing Opinions by Using Declaratively Subjective Clues* Nobuaki Hiroshima, Setsuo Yamada, Osamu Furuse and Ryoji Kataoka
3:30–4:00	Coffee Break
4:00–4:30	*Exploitation in Affect Detection in Open-Ended Improvisational Text* Li Zhang, John A. Barnden, Robert J. Hendley and Alan M. Wallington
4:30–5:00	*Towards a Validated Model for Affective Classification of Texts* Michel Généreux and Roger Evans

Extracting Opinions, Opinion Holders, and Topics Expressed in Online News Media Text

Soo-Min Kim and Eduard Hovy
USC Information Sciences Institute
4676 Admiralty Way
Marina del Rey, CA 90292-6695
{skim, hovy}@ISI.EDU

Abstract

This paper presents a method for identifying an opinion with its holder and topic, given a sentence from online news media texts. We introduce an approach of exploiting the semantic structure of a sentence, anchored to an opinion bearing verb or adjective. This method uses semantic role labeling as an intermediate step to label an opinion holder and topic using data from FrameNet. We decompose our task into three phases: identifying an opinion-bearing word, labeling semantic roles related to the word in the sentence, and then finding the holder and the topic of the opinion word among the labeled semantic roles. For a broader coverage, we also employ a clustering technique to predict the most probable frame for a word which is not defined in FrameNet. Our experimental results show that our system performs significantly better than the baseline.

1 Introduction

The challenge of automatically identifying opinions in text automatically has been the focus of attention in recent years in many different domains such as news articles and product reviews. Various approaches have been adopted in subjectivity detection, semantic orientation detection, review classification and review mining. Despite the successes in identifying opinion expressions and subjective words/phrases, there has been less achievement on the factors closely related to subjectivity and polarity, such as opinion holder, topic of opinion, and inter-topic/inter-opinion relationships. This paper addresses the problem of identifying not only opinions in text but also holders and topics of opinions from online news articles.

Identifying opinion holders is important especially in news articles. Unlike product reviews in which most opinions expressed in a review are likely to be opinions of the author of the review, news articles contain different opinions of different opinion holders (e.g. people, organizations, and countries). By grouping opinion holders of different stance on diverse social and political issues, we can have a better understanding of the relationships among countries or among organizations.

An opinion topic can be considered as an object an opinion is about. In product reviews, for example, opinion topics are often the product itself or its specific features, such as design and quality (e.g. "*I like the design of iPod video*", "*The sound quality is amazing*"). In news articles, opinion topics can be social issues, government's acts, new events, or someone's opinions. (e.g., "*Democrats in Congress accused vice president Dick Cheney's shooting accident.*", "*Shiite leaders accused Sunnis of a mass killing of Shiites in Madaen, south of Baghdad.*")

As for opinion topic identification, little research has been conducted, and only in a very limited domain, product reviews. In most approaches in product review mining, given a product (e.g. mp3 player), its frequently mentioned features (e.g. sound, screen, and design) are first collected and then used as anchor points. In this study, we extract opinion topics from news articles. Also, we do not pre-limit topics in advance. We first identify an opinion and then find its holder and topic. We define *holder* as an entity who holds an opinion, and *topic*, as what the opinion is about.

In this paper, we propose a novel method that employs Semantic Role Labeling, a task of identifying semantic roles given a sentence. We de-

Proceedings of the Workshop on Sentiment and Subjectivity in Text, pages 1–8,
Sydney, July 2006. ©2006 Association for Computational Linguistics

compose the overall task into the following steps:

- Identify opinions.
- Label semantic roles related to the opinions.
- Find holders and topics of opinions among the identified semantic roles.
- Store <opinion, holder, topic> triples into a database.

In this paper, we focus on the first three subtasks.

The main contribution of this paper is to present a method that identifies not only opinion holders but also opinion topics. To achieve this goal, we utilize FrameNet data by mapping target words to opinion-bearing words and mapping semantic roles to holders and topics, and then use them for system training. We demonstrate that investigating semantic relations between an opinion and its holder and topic is crucial in opinion holder and topic identification.

This paper is organized as follows: Section 2 briefly introduces related work both in sentiment analysis and semantic role labeling. Section 3 describes our approach for identifying opinions and labeling holders and topics by utilizing FrameNet[1] data for our task. Section 4 reports our experiments and results with discussions and finally Section 5 concludes.

2 Related Work

This section reviews previous works in both sentiment detection and semantic role labeling.

2.1 Subjectivity and Sentiment Detection

Subjectivity detection is the task of identifying subjective words, expressions, and sentences (Wiebe *et al.*, 1999; Hatzivassiloglou and Wiebe, 2000; Riloff *et al.*, 2003). Identifying subjectivity helps separate opinions from fact, which may be useful in question answering, summarization, etc. Sentiment detection is the task of determining positive or negative sentiment of words (Hatzivassiloglou and McKeown, 1997; Turney, 2002; Esuli and Sebastiani, 2005), phrases and sentences (Kim and Hovy, 2004; Wilson *et al.*, 2005), or documents (Pang *et al.*, 2002; Turney, 2002).

Building on this work, more sophisticated problems such as opinion holder identification have also been studied. (Bethard *et al.*, 2004) identify opinion propositions and holders. Their work is similar to ours but different because their opinion is restricted to propositional opinion and mostly to verbs. Another related works are (Choi *et al.*, 2005; Kim and Hovy, 2005). Both of them use the MPQA corpus[2] but they only identify opinion holders, not topics.

As for opinion topic identification, little research has been conducted, and only in a very limited domain, product reviews. (Hu and Liu, 2004; Popescu and Etzioni, 2005) present product mining algorithms with extracting certain product features given specific product types. Our paper aims at extracting topics of opinion in general news media text.

2.2 Semantic Role Labeling

Semantic role labeling is the task of identifying semantic roles such as Agent, Patient, Speaker, or Topic, in a sentence. A statistical approach for semantic role labeling was introduced by (Gildea and Jurafsky, 2002). Their system learned semantic relationship among constituents in a sentence from FrameNet, a large corpus of semantically hand-annotated data. The FrameNet annotation scheme is based on Frame Semantics (Fillmore, 1976). *Frames* are defined as "schematic representations of situations involving various *frame elements* such as participants, props, and other conceptual roles." For example, given a sentence "Jack built a new house out of bricks", a semantic role labeling system should identify the roles for the verb *built* such as "[$_{\text{Agent}}$ Jack] built [$_{\text{Created\_entity}}$ a new house] [$_{\text{Component}}$ out of bricks]"[3]. In our study, we build a semantic role labeling system as an intermediate step to label opinion holders and topics by training it on opinion-bearing frames and their frame elements in FrameNet.

3 Finding Opinions and Their Holders and Topics

For the goal of this study, extracting opinions from news media texts with their holders and topics, we utilize FrameNet data. The basic idea of our approach is to explore how an opinion holder and a topic are semantically related to an opinion bearing word in a sentence. Given a sentence and an opinion bearing word, our method identifies frame elements in the sentence and

[1] http://framenet.icsi.berkeley.edu/

[2] http://www.cs.pitt.edu/~wiebe/pubs/ardasummer02/

[3] The verb "build" is defined under the frame "Building" in which Agent, Created_entity, and Components are defined as frame elements.

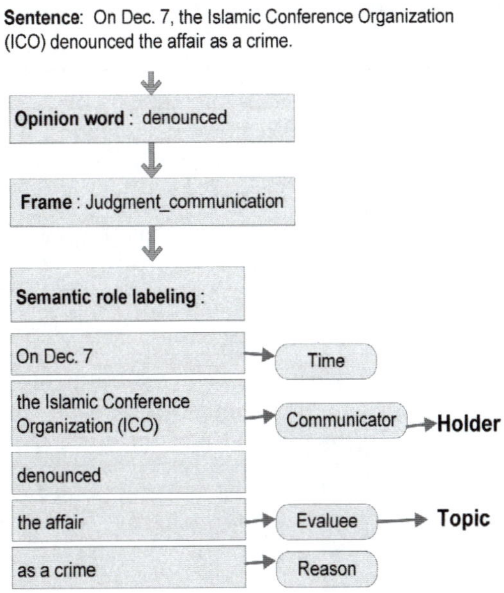

Figure 1: An overview of our algorithm

searches which frame element corresponds to the opinion holder and which to the topic. The example in Figure 1 shows the intuition of our algorithm.

We decompose our task in 3 subtasks: (1) collect opinion words and opinion-related frames, (2) semantic role labeling for those frames, and (3) finally map semantic roles to holder and topic. Following subsections describe each subtask.

3.1 Opinion Words and Related Frames

We describe the subtask of collecting opinion words and related frames in 3 phases.

Phase 1: Collect Opinion Words

In this study, we consider an opinion-bearing (positive/negative) word is a key indicator of an opinion. Therefore, we first identify opinion-bearing word from a given sentence and extract its holder and topic. Since previous studies indicate that opinion-bearing verbs and adjectives are especially efficient for opinion identification, we focus on creating a set of opinion-bearing verbs and adjectives. We annotated 1860 adjectives and 2011 verbs[4] by classifying them into positive, negative, and neutral classes. Words in the positive class carry positive valence whereas those in negative class carry negative valence. Words that are not opinion-bearing are classified as neutral.

Table 1: Example of opinion related frames and lexical units

Frame name	Lexical units	Frame elements
Desiring	want, wish, hope, eager, desire, interested,	Event, Experiencer, Location_of_event
Emotion _directed	agitated, amused, anguish, ashamed, angry, annoyed,	Event, Topic Experiencer, Expressor,
Mental _property	absurd, brilliant, careless, crazy, cunning, foolish	Behavior, Protagonist, Domain, Degree
Subject _stimulus	delightful, amazing, annoying, amusing, aggravating,	Stimulus, Degree Experiencer, Circumstances,

Note that in our study we treat word sentiment classification as a three-way classification problem instead of a two-way classification problem (i.e. positive and negative). By adding the third class, neutral, we can prevent the classifier assigning either positive or negative sentiment to weak opinion-bearing word. For example, the word "central" that Hatzivassiloglou and McKeown (1997) marked as a positive adjective is not classified as positive by our system. Instead we mark it as "neutral", since it is a weak clue for an opinion. For the same reason, we did not consider "able" classified as a positive word by General Inquirer[5], a sentiment word lexicon, as a positive opinion indicator. Finally, we collected 69 positive and 151 negative verbs and 199 positive and 304 negative adjectives.

Phase 2: Find Opinion-related Frames

We collected frames related to opinion words from the FrameNet corpus. We used FrameNet II (Baker *et al.*, 2003) which contains 450 semantic frames and more than 3000 frame elements (FE). A frame consists of lexical items, called *Lexical Unit* (LU), and related frame elements. For instance, LUs in *ATTACK* frame are verbs such as assail, assault, and attack, and nouns such as invasion, raid, and strike. FrameNet II contains

[4] These were randomly selected from 8011 English verbs and 19748 English adjectives.

[5] http://www.wjh.harvard.edu/~inquirer/homecat.htm

approximately 7500 lexical units and over 100,000 annotated sentences.

For each word in our opinion word set described in Phase 1, we find a frame to which the word belongs. 49 frames for verbs and 43 frames for adjectives are collected. Table 1 shows examples of selected frames with some of the lexical units those frames cover. For example, our system found the frame *Desiring* from opinion-bearing words *want, wish, hope, etc.* Finally, we collected 8256 and 11877 sentences related to selected opinion bearing frames for verbs and adjectives respectively.

Phase 3: FrameNet expansion

Even though Phase 2 searches for a correlated frame for each verb and adjective in our opinion-bearing word list, not all of them are defined in FrameNet data. Some words such as *criticize* and *harass* in our list have associated frames (*Case 1*), whereas others such as *vilify* and *maltreat* do not have those (*Case 2*). For a word in Case 2, we use a clustering algorithms CBC (Clustering By Committee) to predict the closest (most reasonable) frame of undefined word from existing frames. CBC (Pantel and Lin, 2002) was developed based on the distributional hypothesis (Harris, 1954) that words which occur in the same contexts tend to be similar. Using CBC, for example, our clustering module computes lexical similarity between the word *vilify* in Case 2 and all words in Case 1. Then it picks *criticize* as a similar word, so that we can use for *vilify* the frame *Judgment_communication* to which *criticize* belongs and all frame elements defined under *Judgment_ communication*.

3.2 Semantic Role Labeling

To find a potential holder and topic of an opinion word in a sentence, we first label semantic roles in a sentence.

Modeling: We follow the statistical approaches for semantic role labeling (Gildea and Jurafsky, 2002; Fleischman *et. al*, 2003) which separate the task into two steps: identify candidates of frame elements (Step 1) and assign semantic roles for those candidates (Step 2). Like their intuition, we treated both steps as classification problems. We first collected all constituents of the given sentence by parsing it using the Charniak parser. Then, in Step 1, we classified candidate constituents of frame elements from non-candidates. In Step 2, each selected candidate was thus classified into one of frame element types (e.g. Stimulus, Degree, Experiencer, etc.). As a learning algorithm for our classification model, we used Maximum Entropy (Berger *et al.*, 1996). For system development, we used MEGA model optimization package[6], an implementation of ME models.

Table 2: Features used for our semantic role labeling model.

Feature	Description
target word	A predicate whose meaning represents the frame (a verb or an adjective in our task)
phrase type	Syntactic type of the frame element (e.g. NP, PP)
head word	Syntactic head of the frame element phrase
parse tree path	A path between the frame element and target word in the parse tree
position	Whether the element phrase occurs *before* or *after* the target word
voice	The voice of the sentence (*active* or *passive*)
frame name	one of our opinion-related frames

Data: We collected 8256 and 11877 sentences which were associated to opinion bearing frames for verbs and adjectives from FrameNet annotation data. Each sentence in our dataset contained a frame name, a target predicate (a word whose meaning represents aspects of the frame), and frame elements labeled with element types. We divided the data into 90% for training and 10% for test.

Features used: Table 2 describes features that we used for our classification model. The target word is an opinion-bearing verb or adjective which is associated to a frame. We used the Charniak parser to get a phrase type feature of a frame element and the parse tree path feature. We determined a head word of a phrase by an algorithm using a tree head table[7], position feature by the order of surface words of a frame element and the target word, and the voice feature by a simple pattern. Frame name for a target

[6] http://www.isi.edu/~hdaume/megam/index.html
[7] http://people.csail.mit.edu/mcollins/papers/heads

Table 3. Precision (P), Recall (R), and *F*-score (F) of Topic and Holder identification for opinion verbs (V) and adjectives (A) on Testset 1.

	Topic			Holder		
	P (%)	R (%)	F (%)	P (%)	R (%)	F (%)
V	69.1	64.0	**66.5**	81.9	75.7	**78.7**
A	67.5	73.4	**70.3**	66.2	77.9	**71.6**

Table 4. Baseline system on Testset 1.

	Topic			Holder		
	P (%)	R (%)	F (%)	P (%)	R (%)	F (%)
V	85.5	18.5	**30.4**	73.7	46.4	**56.9**
A	68.2	26.5	**38.2**	12.0	49.1	**19.3**

word was selected by methods described in Phase 2 and Phase 3 in Subsection 3.1.

3.3 Map Semantic Roles to Holder and Topic

After identifying frame elements in a sentence, our system finally selects holder and topic from those frame elements. In the example in Table 1, the frame "*Desiring*" has frame elements such as Event ("*The change that the Experiencer would like to see*"), Experiencer ("*the person or sentient being who wishes for the Event to occur*"), Location_of_event ("*the place involved in the desired Event*"), Focal_participant ("*entity that the Experiencer wishes to be affected by some Event*"). Among these FEs, we can consider that Experiencer can be a holder and Focal_participant can be a topic (if any exists in a sentence). We manually built a mapping table to map FEs to holder or topic using as support the FE definitions in each opinion related frame and the annotated sample sentences.

4 Experimental Results

The goal of our experiment is first, to see how our holder and topic labeling system works on the FrameNet data, and second, to examine how it performs on online news media text. The first data set (Testset 1) consists of 10% of data described in Subsection 3.2 and the second (Testset 2) is manually annotated by 2 humans. (see Subsection 4.2). We report experimental results for both test sets.

4.1 Experiments on Testset 1

Gold Standard: In total, Testset 1 contains 2028 annotated sentences collected from FrameNet data set. (834 from frames related to opinion verb and 1194 from opinion adjectives) We measure the system performance using precision (the percentage of correct holders/topics among system's labeling results), recall (the percentage of correct holders/topics that system retrieved), and *F*-score.

Baseline: For the baseline system, we applied two different algorithms for sentences which have opinion-bearing verbs as target words and for those that have opinion-bearing adjectives as target words. For **verbs**, baseline system labeled a subject of a verb as a holder and an object as a topic. (e.g. "[$_{\text{holder}}$ He] *condemned* [$_{\text{topic}}$ the lawyer].") For **adjectives**, the baseline marked the subject of a predicate adjective as a holder (e.g. "[$_{\text{holder}}$ I] was *happy*"). For the topics of adjectives, the baseline picks a modified word if the target adjective is a modifier (e.g. "That was a *stupid* [$_{\text{topic}}$ mistake]".) and a subject word if the adjective is a predicate. ([$_{\text{topic}}$ The view] is *breathtaking* in January.)

Result: Table 3 and 4 show evaluation results of our system and the baseline system respectively. Our system performed much better than the baseline system in identifying topic and holder for both sets of sentences with verb target words and those with adjectives. Especially in recognizing topics of target opinion-bearing words, our system improved *F*-score from 30.4% to 66.5% for verb target words and from 38.2% to 70.3% for adjectives. It was interesting to see that the intuition that "*A subject of opinion-bearing verb is a holder and an object is a topic*" which we applied for the baseline achieved relatively good F-score (56.9%). However, our system obtained much higher *F*-score (78.7%). Holder identification task achieved higher *F*-score than topic identification which implies that identifying topics of opinion is a harder task.

We believe that there are many complicated semantic relations between opinion-bearing words and their holders and topics that simple relations such as subject and object relations are not able to capture. For example, in a sentence "Her letter *upset* me", simply looking for the subjective and objective of the verb *upset* is not enough to recognize the holder and topic. It is necessary to see a deeper level of semantic rela-

Table 5. Opinion-bearing sentence identification on Testset 2. (P: precision, R: recall, F: F-score, A: Accuracy, H1: Human1, H2: Human2)

	P (%)	R (%)	F (%)	A (%)
H1	56.9	67.4	61.7	64.0
H2	43.1	57.9	49.4	55.0

Table 6: Results of Topic and Holder identification on Testset 2. (Sys: our system, BL: baseline)

		Topic			Holder		
		P(%)	R(%)	F(%)	P(%)	R(%)	F(%)
Sys	H1	64.7	20.8	31.5	47.9	34.0	39.8
	H2	58.8	7.1	12.7	36.6	26.2	30.5
BL	H1	12.5	9.4	10.7	20.0	28.3	23.4
	H2	23.2	7.1	10.9	14.0	19.0	16.1

tions: "Her letter" is a stimulus and "me" is an experiencer of the verb *upset*.

4.2 Experiments on Testset 2

Gold Standard: Two humans[8] annotated 100 sentences randomly selected from news media texts. Those news data is collected from online news sources such as The New York Times, UN Office for the Coordination of Humanitarian Affairs, and BBC News[9], which contain articles about various international affaires. Annotators identified opinion-bearing sentences with marking opinion word with its holder and topic if they existed. The inter-annotator agreement in identifying opinion sentences was 82%.

Baseline: In order to identify opinion-bearing sentences for our baseline system, we used the opinion-bearing word set introduced in Phase 1 in Subsection 3.1. If a sentence contains an opinion-bearing verb or adjective, the baseline system started looking for its holder and topic. For holder and topic identification, we applied the same baseline algorithm as described in Subsection 4.1 to Testset 2.

Result: Note that Testset 1 was collected from sentences of opinion-related frames in FrameNet and therefore all sentences in the set contained either opinion-bearing verb or adjective. (i.e. All sentences are opinion-bearing) However, sentences in Testset 2 were randomly collected from online news media pages and therefore not all of them are opinion-bearing. We first evaluated the task of opinion-bearing sentence identification. Table 5 shows the system results. When we mark all sentences as opinion-bearing, it achieved 43% and 38% of accuracy for the annotation result of Human1 and Human2 respectively. Our system performance (64% and 55%) is comparable with the unique assignment.

We measured the holder and topic identification system with precision, recall, and *F*-score. As we can see from Table 6, our system achieved much higher precision than the baseline system for both Topic and Holder identification tasks. However, we admit that there is still a lot of room for improvement.

The system achieved higher precision for topic identification, whereas it achieved higher recall for holder identification. In overall, our system attained higher *F*-score in holder identification task, including the baseline system. Based on *F*-score, we believe that identifying topics of opinion is much more difficult than identifying holders. It was interesting to see the same phenomenon that the baseline system mainly assuming that subject and object of a sentence are likely to be opinion holder and topic, achieved lower scores for both holder and topic identification tasks in Testset 2 as in Testset 1. This implies that more sophisticated analysis of the relationship between opinion words (e.g. verbs and adjectives) and their topics and holders is crucial.

4.3 Difficulties in evaluation

We observed several difficulties in evaluating holder and topic identification. First, the boundary of an entity of holder or topic can be flexible. For example, in sentence "Senator Titus Olupitan who sponsored the bill wants the permission.", not only "Senator Titus Olupitan" but also "Senator Titus Olupitan who sponsored the bill" is an eligible answer. Second, some correct holders and topics which our system found were evaluated wrong even if they referred the same entities in the gold standard because human annotators marked only one of them as an answer.

[8] We refer them as Human1 and Human2 for the rest of this paper.
[9] www.nytimes.com, www.irinnews.org, and www.bbc.co.uk

In the future, we need more annotated data for improved evaluation.

5 Conclusion and Future Work

This paper presented a methodology to identify an opinion with its holder and topic given a sentence in online news media texts. We introduced an approach of exploiting semantic structure of a sentence, anchored to an opinion bearing verb or adjective. This method uses semantic role labeling as an intermediate step to label an opinion holder and topic using FrameNet data. Our method first identifies an opinion-bearing word, labels semantic roles related to the word in the sentence, and then finds a holder and a topic of the opinion word among labeled semantic roles.

There has been little previous study in identifying opinion holders and topics partly because it requires a great amount of annotated data. To overcome this barrier, we utilized FrameNet data by mapping target words to opinion-bearing words and mapping semantic roles to holders and topics. However, FrameNet has a limited number of words in its annotated corpus. For a broader coverage, we used a clustering technique to predict a most probable frame for an unseen word.

Our experimental results showed that our system performs significantly better than the baseline. The baseline system results imply that opinion holder and topic identification is a hard task. We believe that there are many complicated semantic relations between opinion-bearing words and their holders and topics which simple relations such as subject and object relations are not able to capture.

In the future, we plan to extend our list of opinion-bearing verbs and adjectives so that we can discover and apply more opinion-related frames. Also, it would be interesting to see how other types of part of speech such as adverbs and nouns affect the performance of the system.

Reference

Baker, Collin F. and Hiroaki Sato. 2003. The FrameNet Data and Software. *Poster and Demonstration at Association for Computational Linguistics*. Sapporo, Japan.

Berger, Adam, Stephen Della Pietra, and Vincent Della Pietra. 1996. A maximum entropy approach to natural language processing, *Computational Linguistics*, (22-1).

Bethard, Steven, Hong Yu, Ashley Thornton, Vasileios Hatzivassiloglou, and Dan Jurafsky. 2004. Automatic Extraction of Opinion Propositions and their Holders, *AAAI Spring Symposium on Exploring Attitude and Affect in Text: Theories and Applications*.

Choi, Y., Cardie, C., Riloff, E., and Patwardhan, S. 2005. Identifying Sources of Opinions with Conditional Random Fields and Extraction Patterns. *Proceedings of HLT/EMNLP-05*.

Esuli, Andrea and Fabrizio Sebastiani. 2005. Determining the semantic orientation of terms through gloss classification. *Proceedings of CIKM-05, 14th ACM International Conference on Information and Knowledge Management*, Bremen, DE, pp. 617-624.

Fillmore, C. Frame semantics and the nature of language. 1976. In *Annals of the New York Academy of Sciences: Conferences on the Origin and Development of Language and Speech*, Volume 280: 20-32.

Fleischman, Michael, Namhee Kwon, and Eduard Hovy. 2003. Maximum Entropy Models for FrameNet Classification. *Proceedings of EMNLP*, Sapporo, Japan.

Gildea, D. and Jurafsky, D. Automatic Labeling of semantic roles. 2002. In *Computational Linguistics*. 28(3), 245-288.

Harris, Zellig, 1954. *Distributional structure*. Word, 10(23) :146--162.

Hatzivassiloglou, Vasileios and Kathleen McKeown. 1997. Predicting the Semantic Orientation of Adjectives. *Proceedings of 35th Annual Meeting of the Assoc. for Computational Linguistics* (ACL-97): 174-181

Hatzivassiloglou, Vasileios and Wiebe, Janyce. 2000. Effects of Adjective Orientation and Gradability on Sentence Subjectivity. *Proceedings of International Conference on Computational Linguistics (COLING-2000)*. Saarbrücken, Germany.

Hu, Minqing and Bing Liu. 2004. Mining and summarizing customer reviews". *Proceedings of the ACM SIGKDD International Conference on Knowledge Discovery & Data Mining (KDD-2004)*, Seattle, Washington, USA.

Kim, Soo-Min and Eduard Hovy. 2004. Determining the Sentiment of Opinions. *Proceedings of COLING-04*. pp. 1367-1373. Geneva, Switzerland.

Kim, Soo-Min and Eduard Hovy. 2005. Identifying Opinion Holders for Question Answering in Opinion Texts. *Proceedings of AAAI-05 Workshop on Question Answering in Restricted Domains*

Pang, Bo, Lillian Lee, and Shivakumar Vaithyanathan. 2002. Thumbs up? Sentiment Classification using Machine Learning Techniques, *Proceedings of EMNLP*-2002.

Pantel, Patrick and Dekang Lin. 2002. Discovering Word Senses from Text. *Proceedings of ACM Conference on Knowledge Discovery and Data Mining. (KDD-02)*. pp. 613-619. Edmonton, Canada.

Popescu, Ana-Maria and Oren Etzioni. 2005. Extracting Product Features and Opinions from Reviews , *Proceedings of HLT-EMNLP* 2005.

Riloff, Ellen, Janyce Wiebe, and Theresa Wilson. 2003. Learning Subjective Nouns Using Extraction Pattern Bootstrapping. *Proceedings of Seventh Conference on Natural Language Learning (CoNLL-03)*. ACL SIGNLL. Pages 25-32.

Turney, Peter D. 2002. Thumbs up or thumbs down? Semantic orientation applied to unsupervised classification of reviews, *Proceedings of ACL-02*, Philadelphia, Pennsylvania, 417-424

Wiebe, Janyce, Bruce M., Rebecca F., and Thomas P. O'Hara. 1999. Development and use of a gold standard data set for subjectivity classifications. *Proceedings of ACL-99*. University of Maryland, June, pp. 246-253.

Wilson, Theresa, Janyce Wiebe, and Paul Hoffmann. 2005. Recognizing Contextual Polarity in Phrase-Level Sentiment Analysis. *Proceedings of HLT/EMNLP 2005*, Vancouver, Canada

Toward Opinion Summarization: Linking the Sources

Veselin Stoyanov and **Claire Cardie**
Department of Computer Science
Cornell University
Ithaca, NY 14850, USA
{ves,cardie}@cs.cornell.edu

Abstract

We target the problem of linking source mentions that belong to the same entity (source coreference resolution), which is needed for creating opinion summaries. In this paper we describe how source coreference resolution can be transformed into standard noun phrase coreference resolution, apply a state-of-the-art coreference resolution approach to the transformed data, and evaluate on an available corpus of manually annotated opinions.

1 Introduction

Sentiment analysis is concerned with the extraction and representation of attitudes, evaluations, opinions, and sentiment from text. The area of sentiment analysis has been the subject of much recent research interest driven by two primary motivations. First, there is a desire to provide applications that can extract, represent, and allow the exploration of opinions in the commercial, government, and political domains. Second, effective sentiment analysis might be used to enhance and improve existing NLP applications such as information extraction, question answering, summarization, and clustering (e.g. Riloff et al. (2005), Stoyanov et al. (2005)).

Several research efforts (e.g. Riloff and Wiebe (2003), Bethard et al. (2004), Wilson et al. (2004), Yu and Hatzivassiloglou (2003), Wiebe and Riloff (2005)) have shown that sentiment information can be extracted at the sentence, clause, or individual opinion expression level (*fine-grained opinion information*). However, little has been done to develop methods for combining fine-grained opinion information to form a summary representation in which expressions of opinions from the same source/target[1] are grouped together, multiple opinions from a source toward the same target are accumulated into an aggregated opinion, and cumulative statistics are computed for each source/target. A simple opinion summary[2] is shown in Figure 1. Being able to create opinion summaries is important both for stand-alone applications of sentiment analysis as well as for the potential uses of sentiment analysis as part of other NLP applications.

In this work we address the dearth of approaches for summarizing opinion information. In particular, we focus on the problem of *source coreference resolution*, i.e. deciding which source mentions are associated with opinions that belong to the same real-world entity. In the example from Figure 1 performing source coreference resolution amounts to determining that *Stanishev*, *he*, and *he* refer to the same real-world entities. Given the associated opinion expressions and their polarity, this source coreference information is the critical knowledge needed to produce the summary of Figure 1 (although the two target mentions, *Bulgaria* and *our country*, would also need to be identified as coreferent).

Our work is concerned with fine-grained expressions of opinions and assumes that a system can rely on the results of effective opinion and source extractors such as those described in Riloff and Wiebe (2003), Bethard et al. (2004), Wiebe and Riloff (2005) and Choi et al. (2005). Presented with sources of opinions, we approach the problem of source coreference resolution as the closely

[1] We use *source* to denote an opinion holder and *target* to denote the entity toward which the opinion is directed.

[2] For simplicity, the example summary does not contain any source/target statistics or combination of multiple opinions from the same source to the same target.

Proceedings of the Workshop on Sentiment and Subjectivity in Text, pages 9–14,
Sydney, July 2006.

" [$_{\text{Target}}$ Delaying of Bulgaria's accession to the EU] would be a *serious mistake*" [$_{\text{Source}}$ Bulgarian Prime Minister Sergey Stanishev] said in an interview for the German daily Suddeutsche Zeitung. "[$_{\text{Target}}$ Our country] *serves as a model and encourages* countries from the region to follow despite the difficulties", [$_{\text{Source}}$ he] added.

[$_{\text{Target}}$ Bulgaria] is *criticized* by [$_{\text{Source}}$ the EU] because of slow reforms in the judiciary branch, the newspaper notes.

Stanishev was elected prime minister in 2005. Since then, [$_{\text{Source}}$ he] has been a *prominent supporter* of [$_{\text{Target}}$ his country's accession to the EU].

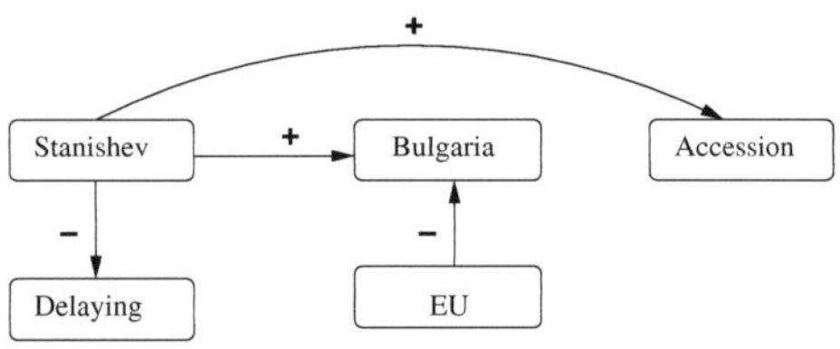

Figure 1: Example of text containing opinions (above) and a summary of the opinions (below). In the text, sources and targets of opinions are marked and opinion expressions are shown in italic. In the summary graph, + stands for positive opinion and - for negative.

related task of noun phrase coreference resolution. However, source coreference resolution differs from traditional noun phrase (NP) coreference resolution in two important aspects discussed in Section 4. Nevertheless, as a first attempt at source coreference resolution, we employ a state-of-the-art machine learning approach to NP coreference resolution developed by Ng and Cardie (2002). Using a corpus of manually annotated opinions, we perform an extensive evaluation and obtain strong initial results for the task of source coreference resolution.

2 Related Work

Sentiment analysis has been a subject of much recent research. Several efforts have attempted to automatically extract opinions, emotions, and sentiment from text. The problem of sentiment extraction at the document level (*sentiment classification*) has been tackled as a text categorization task in which the goal is to assign to a document either positive ("thumbs up") or negative ("thumbs down") polarity (e.g. Das and Chen (2001), Pang et al. (2002), Turney (2002), Dave et al. (2003), Pang and Lee (2004)). In contrast, the problem of fine-grained opinion extraction has concentrated on recognizing opinions at the sentence, clause, or individual opinion expression level. Recent work has shown that systems can be trained to recognize opinions, their polarity, and their strength at a reasonable degree of accuracy (e.g. Dave et al. (2003), Riloff and Wiebe (2003), Bethard et al. (2004), Pang and Lee (2004), Wilson et al. (2004), Yu and Hatzivassiloglou (2003), Wiebe and Riloff (2005)). Additionally, researchers have been able to effectively identify sources of opinions automatically (Bethard et al., 2004; Choi et al., 2005; Kim and Hovy, 2005). Finally, Liu et al. (2005) summarize automatically generated opinions about products and develop interface that allows the summaries to be vizualized.

Our work also draws on previous work in the area of coreference resolution, which is a relatively well studied NLP problem. Coreference resolution is the problem of deciding what noun phrases in the text (i.e. *mentions*) refer to the same real-world entities (i.e. *are coreferent*). Generally, successful approaches have relied machine learning methods trained on a corpus of documents annotated with coreference information (such as the MUC and ACE corpora). Our approach to source coreference resolution is inspired by the state-of-the-art performance of the method of Ng and Cardie (2002).

3 Data set

We begin our discussion by describing the data set that we use for development and evaluation.

As noted previously, we desire methods that work with automatically identified opinions and sources. However, for the purpose of developing and evaluating our approaches we rely on a corpus of manually annotated opinions and sources. More precisely, we rely on the MPQA corpus (Wilson and Wiebe, 2003)[3], which contains 535 manually annotated documents. Full details about the corpus and the process of corpus creation can be found in Wilson and Wiebe (2003); full details of the opinion annotation scheme can be found in Wiebe et al. (2005). For the purposes of the discussion in this paper, the following three points suffice.

First, the corpus is suitable for the domains and genres that we target – all documents have occurred in the world press over an 11-month period, between June 2001 and May 2002. Therefore, the

[3]The MPQA corpus is available at `http://nrrc.mitre.org/NRRC/publications.htm`.

corpus is suitable for the political and government domains as well as a substantial part of the commercial domain. However, a fair portion of the commercial domain is concerned with opinion extraction from product reviews. Work described in this paper does not target the genre of reviews, which appears to differ significantly from newspaper articles.

Second, all documents are manually annotated with phrase-level opinion information. The annotation scheme of Wiebe et al. (2005) includes phrase level opinions, their sources, as well as other attributes, which are not utilized by our approach. Additionally, the annotations contain information that allows coreference among source mentions to be recovered.

Finally, the MPQA corpus contains no coreference information for general NPs (which are not sources). This might present a problem for traditional coreference resolution approaches, as discussed throughout the paper.

4 Source Coreference Resolution

In this Section we define the problem of source coreference resolution, describe its challenges, and provide an overview of our general approach.

We define *source coreference resolution* as the problem of determining which mentions of opinion sources refer to the same real-world entity. Source coreference resolution differs from traditional supervised NP coreference resolution in two important aspects. First, sources of opinions do not exactly correspond to the automatic extractors' notion of noun phrases (NPs). Second, due mainly to the time-consuming nature of coreference annotation, NP coreference information is incomplete in our data set: NP mentions that are not sources of opinion are not annotated with coreference information (even when they are part of a chain that contains source NPs)[4]. In this paper we address the former problem via a heuristic method for mapping sources to NPs and give statistics for the accuracy of the mapping process. We then apply state-of-the-art coreference resolution methods to the NPs to which sources were mapped (*source noun phrases*). The latter problem of developing methods that can work with incomplete supervisory information is addressed in a subsequent effort (Stoyanov and Cardie, 2006).

[4]This problem is illustrated in the example of Figure 1 The underlined *Stanishev* is coreferent with all of the Stanishev references marked as sources, but, because it is used in an objective sentence rather than as the source of an opinion, the reference would be omitted from the *Stanishev* source coreference chain. Unfortunately, this proper noun might be critical in establishing coreference of the final source reference *he* with the other mentions of the source *Stanishev*.

	Single Match	Multiple Matches	No Match
Total	7811	3461	50
Exact	6242	1303	0

Table 1: Statistics for matching sources to noun phrases.

Our general approach to source coreference resolution consists of the following steps:

1. **Preprocessing:** We preprocess the corpus by running NLP components such as a tokenizer, sentence splitter, POS tagger, parser, and a base NP finder. Subsequently, we augment the set of the base NPs found by the base NP finder with the help of a named entity finder. The preprocessing is done following the NP coreference work by Ng and Cardie (2002). From the preprocessing step, we obtain an augmented set of NPs in the text.
2. **Source to noun phrase mapping:** The problem of mapping (manually or automatically annotated) sources to NPs is not trivial. We map sources to NPs using a set of heuristics.
3. **Coreference resolution:** Finally, we restrict our attention to the source NPs identified in step 2. We extract a feature vector for every pair of source NPs from the preprocessed corpus and perform NP coreference resolution.

The next two sections give the details of Steps 2 and 3, respectively. We follow with the results of an evaluation of our approach in Section 7.

5 Mapping sources to noun phrases

This section describes our method for heuristically mapping sources to NPs. In the context of source coreference resolution we consider a noun phrase to correspond to (or match) a source if the source and the NP cover the exact same span of text. Unfortunately, the annotated sources did not always match exactly a single automatically extracted NP. We discovered the following problems:

1. **Inexact span match.** We discovered that often (in 3777 out of the 11322 source mentions) there is no noun phrase whose span matches exactly the source although there are noun phrases that overlap the source. In most cases this is due to the way spans of sources are marked in the data. For instance, in some cases determiners are not included in the source span (e.g. "*Venezuelan people*" vs. "*the Venezuelan people*"). In other cases, differences are due to mistakes by the NP extractor (e.g. "*Muslims rulers*" was not recognized, while "*Muslims*" and "*rulers*" were recognized). Yet in other cases, manually marked sources do not match the definition of a noun phrase. This case is described in more detail next.

	Measure	Overall rank	Method and parameters	Instance selection	B^3	MUC score	Positive Identification			Actual Pos. Identification		
							Prec.	Recall	F1	Prec.	Recall	F1
400 Training Documents	B^3	1	svm C10 γ0.01	none	**81.8**	71.7	80.2	43.7	56.6	57.5	62.9	60.2
		5	ripper asc L2	soon2	**80.7**	72.2	74.5	45.2	56.3	55.1	62.1	58.4
	MUC Score	1	svm C10 γ0.01	soon1	77.3	**74.2**	67.4	51.7	58.5	37.8	70.9	49.3
		4	ripper acs L1.5	soon2	78.4	**73.6**	68.3	49.0	57.0	40.0	69.9	50.9
	Positive identification	1	svm C10 γ0.05	soon1	72.7	73.9	60.0	57.2	**58.6**	37.8	71.0	49.3
		4	ripper acs L1.5	soon1	78.9	73.6	68.8	48.9	**57.2**	40.0	69.9	50.9
	Actual pos. identification	1	svm C10 γ0.01	none	81.8	71.7	80.2	43.7	56.6	57.5	62.9	**60.2**
		2	ripper asc L4	soon2	73.9	69.9	81.1	40.2	53.9	69.8	52.5	**60.0**
200 Training Documents	B^3	1	ripper acs L4	none	**81.8**	67.8	91.4	32.7	48.2	72.0	52.5	60.6
		9	svm C10 γ0.01	none	**81.4**	70.3	81.6	40.8	54.4	58.4	61.6	59.9
	MUC Score	1	svm C1 γ0.1	soon1	74.8	**73.8**	63.2	55.2	58.9	32.1	74.4	44.9
		5	ripper acs L1	soon1	77.9	**0.732**	71.4	46.5	56.3	37.7	69.7	48.9
	Positive identification	1	svm C1 γ0.1	soon1	74.8	73.8	63.2	55.2	**58.9**	32.1	74.4	44.9
		4	ripper acs L1	soon1	75.3	72.4	69.1	48.0	**56.7**	33.3	72.3	45.6
	Actual pos. identification	1	ripper acs L4	none	81.8	67.8	91.4	32.7	48.2	72.0	52.5	**60.6**
		10	svm C10 γ0.01	none	81.4	70.3	81.6	40.8	54.4	58.4	61.6	**59.9**

Table 2: Performance of the best runs. For SVMs, γ stands for RBF kernel with the shown γ parameter.

2. **Multiple NP match.** For 3461 of the 11322 source mentions more than one NP overlaps the source. In roughly a quarter of these cases the multiple match is due to the presence of nested NPs (introduced by the NP augmentation process introduced in Section 3). In other cases the multiple match is caused by source annotations that spanned multiple NPs or included more than only NPs inside its span. There are three general classes of such sources. First, some of the marked sources are appositives such as "*the country's new president, Eduardo Duhalde*". Second, some sources contain an NP followed by an attached prepositional phrase such as "*Latin American leaders at a summit meeting in Costa Rica*". Third, some sources are conjunctions of NPs such as "*Britain, Canada and Australia*". Treatment of the latter is still a controversial problem in the context of coreference resolution as it is unclear whether conjunctions represent entities that are distinct from the conjuncts. For the purpose of our current work we do not attempt to address conjunctions.

3. **No matching NP.** Finally, for 50 of the 11322 sources there are no overlapping NPs. Half of those (25 to be exact) included marking of the word "*who*" such as in the sentence "*Carmona named new ministers, including two military officers* **who** *rebelled against Chavez*". From the other 25, 19 included markings of non-NPs including question words, qualifiers, and adjectives such as "*many*", "*which*", and "*domestically*". The remaining six are rare NPs such as "*lash*" and "*taskforce*" that are mistakenly not recognized by the NP extractor.

Counts for the different types of matches of sources to NPs are shown in Table 1. We determine the match in the problematic cases using a set of heuristics:

1. If a source matches any NP exactly in span, match that source to the NP; do this even if multiple NPs overlap the source – we are dealing with nested NP's.

2. If no NP matches matches exactly in span then:
   - If a single NP overlaps the source, then map the source to that NP. Most likely we are dealing with differently marked spans.
   - If multiple NPs overlap the source, determine whether the set of overlapping NPs include any non-nested NPs. If all overlapping NPs are nested with each other, select the NP that is closer in span to the source – we are still dealing with differently marked spans, but now we also have nested NPs. If there is more than one set of nested NPs, then most likely the source spans more than a single NP. In this case we select the outermost of the last set of nested NPs before any preposition in the span. We prefer: the outermost NP because longer NPs contain more information; the last NP because it is likely to be the head NP of a phrase (also handles the case of explanation followed by a proper noun); NP's before preposition, because a preposition signals an explanatory prepositional phrase.

3. If no NP overlaps the source, select the last NP before the source. In half of the cases we are dealing with the word *who*, which typically refers to the last preceding NP.

6 Source coreference resolution as coreference resolution

Once we isolate the source NPs, we apply coreference resolution using the standard combination of classification and single-link clustering (e.g. Soon et al. (2001) and Ng and Cardie (2002)).

We compute a vector of 57 features for every pair of source noun phrases from the preprocessed corpus. We use the training set of pairwise instances to train a classifier to predict whether a source NP pair should be classified as positive (the NPs refer to the same entity) or negative (different entities). During testing, we use the trained classifier to predict whether a source NP pair is positive and single-link clustering to group together sources that belong to the same entity.

7 Evaluation

For evaluation we randomly split the MPQA corpus into a training set consisting of 400 documents and a test set consisting of the remaining 135 documents. We use the same test set for all evaluations, although not all runs were trained on all 400 training documents as discussed below.

The purpose of our evaluation is to create a strong baseline utilizing the best settings for the NP coreference approach. As such, we try the two reportedly best machine learning techniques for pairwise classification – RIPPER (for Repeated Incremental Pruning to Produce Error Reduction) (Cohen, 1995) and support vector machines (SVMs) in the SVM^{light} implementation (Joachims, 1998). Additionally, to exclude possible effects of parameter selection, we try many different parameter settings for the two classifiers. For RIPPER we vary the order of classes and the positive/negative weight ratio. For SVMs we vary C (the margin tradeoff) and the type and parameter of the kernel. In total, we use 24 different settings for RIPPER and 56 for SVM^{light}.

Additionally, Ng and Cardie reported better results when the training data distribution is balanced through instance selection. For instance selection they adopt the method of Soon et al. (2001), which selects for each NP the pairs with the n preceding coreferent instances and all intervening non-coreferent pairs. Following Ng and Cardie (2002), we perform instance selection with $n = 1$ ($soon1$ in the results) and $n = 2$ ($soon2$). With the three different instance selection algorithms ($soon1$, $soon2$, and none), the total number of settings is 72 for RIPPER and 168 for SVMa. However, not all SVM runs completed in the time limit that we set – 200 min, so we selected half of the training set (200 documents) at random and trained all classifiers on that set. We made sure to run to completion on the full training set those SVM settings that produced the best results on the smaller training set.

Table 2 lists the results of the best performing runs. The upper half of the table gives the results for the runs that were trained on 400 documents and the lower half contains the results for the 200-document training set. We evaluated using the two widely used performance measures for coreference resolution – MUC score (Vilain et al., 1995) and B^3 (Bagga and Baldwin, 1998). In addition, we used performance metrics (precision, recall and F1) on the identification of the positive class. We compute the latter in two different ways – either by using the pairwise decisions as the classifiers outputs them or by performing the clustering of the source NPs and then considering a pairwise decision to be positive if the two source NPs belong to the same cluster. The second option (marked *actual* in Table 2) should be more representative of a good clustering, since coreference decisions are important only in the context of the clusters that they create.

Table 2 shows the performance of the best RIPPER and SVM runs for each of the four evaluation metrics. The table also lists the rank for each run among the rest of the runs.

7.1 Discussion

The absolute B^3 and MUC scores for source coreference resolution are comparable to reported state-of-the-art results for NP coreference resolutions. Results should be interpreted cautiously, however, due to the different characteristics of our data. Our documents contained 35.34 source NPs per document on average, with coreference chains consisting of only 2.77 NPs on average. The low average number of NPs per chain may be producing artificially high score for the B^3 and MUC scores as the modest results on positive class identification indicate.

From the relative performance of our runs, we observe the following trends. First, SVMs trained on the full training set outperform RIPPER trained on the same training set as well as the corresponding SVMs trained on the 200-document training set. The RIPPER runs exhibit the opposite behavior – RIPPER outperforms SVMs on the 200-document training set and RIPPER runs trained on the smaller data set exhibit better performance. Overall, the single best performance is observed by RIPPER using the smaller training set.

Another interesting observation is that the B^3 measure correlates well with good "actual" performance on positive class identification. In contrast, good MUC performance is associated with runs that exhibit high recall on the positive class. This confirms some theoretical concerns that MUC score does not reward algorithms that recognize well the absence of links. In addition, the results confirm our conjecture that "actual" precision and recall are more indicative of the true performance of coreference algorithms.

8 Conclusions

As a first step toward opinion summarization we targeted the problem of source coreference resolution. We showed that the problem can be tackled effectively as noun coreference resolution.

One aspect of source coreference resolution that we do not address is the use of unsupervised information. The corpus contains many automatically identified non-source NPs, which can be used to benefit source coreference resolution in two ways. First, a machine learning approach could use the unlabeled data to estimate the overall distributions. Second, some links between sources may be realized through a non-source NPs (see the example of figure 1). As a follow-up to the work described in this paper we developed a method that utilizes the unlabeled NPs in the corpus using a structured rule learner (Stoyanov and Cardie, 2006).

Acknowledgements

The authors would like to thank Vincent Ng and Art Munson for providing coreference resolution code, members of the Cornell NLP group (especially Yejin Choi and Art Munson) for many helpful discussions, and the anonymous reviewers for their insightful comments. This work was supported by the Advanced Research and Development Activity (ARDA), by NSF Grants IIS-0535099 and IIS-0208028, by gifts from Google and the Xerox Foundation, and by an NSF Graduate Research Fellowship to the first author.

References

A. Bagga and B. Baldwin. 1998. Entity-based cross-document coreferencing using the vector space model. In *Proceedings of COLING/ACL*.

S. Bethard, H. Yu, A. Thornton, V. Hativassiloglou, and D. Jurafsky. 2004. Automatic extraction of opinion propositions and their holders. In *2004 AAAI Spring Symposium on Exploring Attitude and Affect in Text*.

Y. Choi, C. Cardie, E. Riloff, and S. Patwardhan. 2005. Identifying sources of opinions with conditional random fields and extraction patterns. In *Proceedings of EMNLP*.

W. Cohen. 1995. Fast effective rule induction. In *Proceedings of ICML*.

S. Das and M. Chen. 2001. Yahoo for amazon: Extracting market sentiment from stock message boards. In *Proceedings of APFAAC*.

K. Dave, S. Lawrence, and D. Pennock. 2003. Mining the peanut gallery: Opinion extraction and semantic classification of product reviews. In *Proceedings of IWWWC*.

T. Joachims. 1998. Making large-scale support vector machine learning practical. In A. Smola B. Schölkopf, C. Burges, editor, *Advances in Kernel Methods: Support Vector Machines*. MIT Press, Cambridge, MA.

S. Kim and E. Hovy. 2005. Identifying opinion holders for question answering in opinion texts. In *Proceedings of AAAI Workshop on Question Answering in Restricted Domains*.

B. Liu, M. Hu, and J. Cheng. 2005. Opinion observer: Analyzing and comparing opinions on the web. In *Proceedings of International World Wide Web Conference*.

V. Ng and C. Cardie. 2002. Improving machine learning approaches to coreference resolution. In *Proceedings of ACL*.

B. Pang and L. Lee. 2004. A sentimental education: Sentiment analysis using subjectivity summarization based on minimum cuts. In *Proceedings of ACL*.

B. Pang, L. Lee, and S. Vaithyanathan. 2002. Thumbs up? Sentiment classification using machine learning techniques. In *Proceedings of EMNLP*.

E. Riloff and J. Wiebe. 2003. Learning extraction patterns for subjective expressions. In *Proceesings of EMNLP*.

E. Riloff, J. Wiebe, and W. Phillips. 2005. Exploiting subjectivity classification to improve information extraction. In *Proceedings of AAAI*.

W. Soon, H. Ng, and D. Lim. 2001. A machine learning approach to coreference resolution of noun phrases. *Computational Linguistics*, 27(4).

V. Stoyanov and C. Cardie. 2006. Partially supervised coreference resolution for opinion summarization through structured rule learning. In *Proceedings of EMNLP*.

V. Stoyanov, C. Cardie, and J. Wiebe. 2005. Multi-Perspective question answering using the OpQA corpus. In *Proceedings of EMNLP*.

P. Turney. 2002. Thumbs up or thumbs down? Semantic orientation applied to unsupervised classification of reviews. In *Proceedings of ACL*.

M. Vilain, J. Burger, J. Aberdeen, D. Connolly, and L. Hirschman. 1995. A model-theoretic coreference scoring scheme. In *Proceedings of MUC-6*.

J. Wiebe and E. Riloff. 2005. Creating subjective and objective sentence classifiers from unannotated texts. In *Proceedings of CICLing*.

J. Wiebe, T. Wilson, and C. Cardie. 2005. Annotating expressions of opinions and emotions in language. *Language Resources and Evaluation*, 1(2).

T. Wilson and J. Wiebe. 2003. Annotating opinions in the world press. *4th SIGdial Workshop on Discourse and Dialogue (SIGdial-03)*.

T. Wilson, J. Wiebe, and R. Hwa. 2004. Just how mad are you? Finding strong and weak opinion clauses. In *Proceedings of AAAI*.

H. Yu and V. Hatzivassiloglou. 2003. Towards answering opinion questions: Separating facts from opinions and identifying the polarity of opinion sentences. In *Proceedings of EMNLP*.

A System for Summarizing and Visualizing Arguments in Subjective Documents: Toward Supporting Decision Making

Atsushi Fujii
Graduate School of Library,
Information and Media Studies
University of Tsukuba
1-2 Kasuga, Tsukuba, 305-8550, Japan
fujii@slis.tsukuba.ac.jp

Tetsuya Ishikawa
The Historiographical Institute
The University of Tokyo
3-1 Hongo 7-chome, Bunkyo-ku
Tokyo, 133-0033, Japan
ishikawa@hi.u-tokyo.ac.jp

Abstract

On the World Wide Web, the volume of subjective information, such as opinions and reviews, has been increasing rapidly. The trends and rules latent in a large set of subjective descriptions can potentially be useful for decision-making purposes. In this paper, we propose a method for summarizing subjective descriptions, specifically opinions in Japanese. We visualize the pro and con arguments for a target topic, such as "Should Japan introduce the summertime system?" Users can summarize the arguments about the topic in order to choose a more reasonable standpoint for decision making. We evaluate our system, called "OpinionReader", experimentally.

1 Introduction

On the World Wide Web, users can easily disseminate information irrespective of their own specialty. Thus, natural language information on the Web is not restricted to objective and authorized information, such as news stories and technical publications. The volume of subjective information, such as opinions and reviews, has also been increasing rapidly.

Although a single subjective description by an anonymous author is not always reliable, the trends and rules latent in a large set of subjective descriptions can potentially be useful for decision-making purposes.

In one scenario, a user may read customer reviews before choosing a product. In another scenario, a user may assess the pros and cons of a political issue before determining their own attitude on the issue.

The decision making in the above scenarios is performed according to the following processes:

(1) collecting documents related to a specific topic from the Web;
(2) extracting subjective descriptions from the documents;
(3) classifying the subjective descriptions according to their polarity, such as positive/negative or pro/con;
(4) organizing (e.g., summarizing and/or visualizing) the classified descriptions so that users can view important points selectively;
(5) making the decision.

Because it is expensive to perform all of the above processes manually, a number of automatic methods have been explored. Specifically, a large number of methods have been proposed to facilitate processes (2) and (3).

In this paper, we focus on process (4), and propose a method for summarizing subjective information, specifically opinions in Japanese. Our method visualizes the pro and con arguments for a target topic, such as "Should Japan introduce the summertime system?"

By process (4), users can summarize the arguments about the topic in order to choose a more reasonable standpoint on it. Consequently, our system supports decision making by users.

However, process (5) is beyond the scope of this paper, and remains an intellectual activity for human beings.

We describe and demonstrate our prototype system, called "OpinionReader". We also evaluate the components of our system experimentally.

Section 2 surveys previous research on the processing of subjective information. Section 3 provides an overview of OpinionReader, and Sec-

Proceedings of the Workshop on Sentiment and Subjectivity in Text, pages 15–22,
Sydney, July 2006.

tion 4 describes the methodologies of its components. Section 5 describes the experiments and discusses the results obtained.

2 Related Work

For process (1) in Section 1, existing search engines can be used to search the Web for documents related to a specific topic. However, not all retrieved documents include subjective descriptions for the topic.

A solution to this problem is to automatically identify diaries and blogs (Nanno et al., 2004), which usually include opinionated subjective descriptions.

For process (2), existing methods aim to distinguish between subjective and objective descriptions in texts (Kim and Hovy, 2004; Pang and Lee, 2004; Riloff and Wiebe, 2003).

For process (3), machine-learning methods are usually used to classify subjective descriptions into bipolar categories (Dave et al., 2003; Beineke et al., 2004; Hu and Liu, 2004; Pang and Lee, 2004) or multipoint scale categories (Kim and Hovy, 2004; Pang and Lee, 2005).

For process (4), which is the subject of this paper, Ku et al. (2005) selected documents that include a large number of positive or negative sentences about a target topic, and used their headlines as a summary of the topic. This is the application of an existing extraction-based summarization method to subjective descriptions.

Hu and Liu (2004) summarized customer reviews of a product such as a digital camera. Their summarization method extracts nouns and noun phrases as features of the target product, (e.g., "picture" for a digital camera), and lists positive and negative reviews on a feature-by-feature basis.

The extracted features are sorted according to the frequency with which each feature appears in the reviews. This method allows users to browse the reviews in terms of important features of the target product.

Liu et al. (2005) enhanced the above method to allow users to compare different products within a specific category, on a feature-by-feature basis.

3 Overview of OpinionReader

Figure 1 depicts the process flow in OpinionReader. The input is a set of subjective descriptions for a specific topic, classified according to their polarity. We assume that processes (1)–(3) in Section 1 are completed, either manually or automatically, prior to the use of our system. It is often the case that users post their opinions and state their standpoints, as exemplified by the websites used in our experiments (see Section 5).

While our primarily target is a set of opinions for a debatable issue classified into pros and cons, a set of customer reviews for a product, classified as positive or negative, can also be submitted.

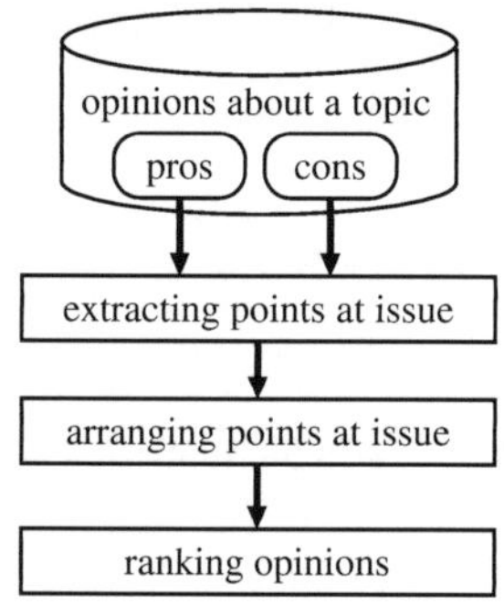

Figure 1: Process flow in OpinionReader.

Our purpose is to visualize the pro and con arguments about a target topic, so that a user can determine which standpoint is the more reasonable.

We extract "points at issue" from the opinions and arrange them in a two-dimensional space. We also rank the opinions that include each point at issue according to their importance, so that a user can selectively read representative opinions on a point-by-point basis.

The output is presented via a graphical interface as shown in Figure 2, which is an example output for the topic "privatization of hospitals by joint-stock companies". The opinions used for this example are extracted from the website for "BS debate"[1]. This interface is accessible via existing Web browsers.

In Figure 2, the x and y axes correspond to the polarity and importance respectively, and each oval denotes an extracted point at issue, such as "information disclosure", "health insurance", or "medical corporation".

Users can easily see which points at issue are most important from each standpoint. Points at issue that are important and closely related to one particular standpoint are usually the most useful in users' decision making.

By clicking on an oval in Figure 2, users can read representative opinions corresponding to that

[1] http://www.nhk.or.jp/bsdebate/

point at issue. In Figure 3, two opinions that include "information disclosure" are presented. The opinions on the right and left sides are selected from the pros and cons, respectively. While the pros support information disclosure, the cons insist that they have not recognized its necessity.

As a result, users can browse the pro and con arguments about the topic in detail. However, for some points at issue, only opinions from a single standpoint are presented, because the other side has no argument about that point.

Given the above functions, users can easily summarize the main points and how they are used in arguing about the topic in support of one standpoint or the other.

If subjective descriptions are classified into more than two categories with a single axis, we can incorporate these descriptions into our system by reclassifying them into just two categories. Figure 4 is an example of summarizing reviews with a multipoint scale rating. We used reviews with five-point star rating for the movie "Star Wars: Episode III"[2]. We reclassified reviews with 1–3 stars as cons, and reviews with 4–5 stars as pros.

In Figure 4, the points at issue are typical words used in the movie reviews (e.g. "story"), the names of characters (e.g. "Anakin", "Obi-Wan", and "Palpatine"), concepts related to Star Wars (e.g. "battle scene" and "Dark Side"), and comparisons with other movies (e.g., "War of the Worlds").

Existing methods for summarizing opinions (Hu and Liu, 2004; Liu et al., 2005). extract the features of a product, which corresponds to the points at issue in our system, and arrange them along a single dimension representing the importance of features. The reviews corresponding to each feature are not ranked.

However, in our system, features are arranged to show how the feature relates to each polarity. The opinions addressing a feature are ranked according to their importance. We target both opinions and reviews, as shown in Figures 2 and 4, respectively.

4 Methodology

4.1 Extracting Points at Issue

In a preliminary investigation of political opinions on the Web, we identified that points at issue can be different language units: words, phrases, sentences, and combinations of sentences. We currently target nouns, noun phrases, and verb phrases, whereas existing summarization methods (Hu and Liu, 2004; Liu et al., 2005) extract only nouns and noun phrases.

Because Japanese sentences lack lexical segmentation, we first use ChaSen[3] to perform a morphological analysis of each input sentence. As a result, we can identify the words in the input and their parts of speech.

To extract nouns and noun phrases, we use handcrafted rules that rely on the word and part-of-speech information. We extract words and word sequences that match these rules. To standardize among the different noun phrases that describe the same content, we paraphrase specific types of noun phrases.

To extract verb phrases, we analyze the syntactic dependency structure of each input sentence, by using CaboCha[4]. We then use handcrafted rules to extract verb phrases comprising a noun and a verb from the dependency structure.

It is desirable that the case of a noun (i.e., postpositional particles) and the modality of a verb (i.e., auxiliaries) are maintained. However, if we were to allow variations of case and modality, verb phrases related to almost the same meaning would be regarded as different points at issue and thus the output of our system would contain redundancy. Therefore, for the sake of conciseness, we currently discard postpositional particles and auxiliaries in verb phrases.

4.2 Arranging Points at Issue

In our system, the points at issue extracted as described in Section 4.1 are arranged in a two-dimensional space, as shown in Figure 2. The x-axis corresponds to the polarity of the points at issue, that is the degree to which a point is related to each standpoint. The y-axis corresponds to the importance of the points at issue.

For a point at issue A, which can be a noun, noun phrase, or verb phrase, the x-coordinate, x_A, is calculated by Equation (1):

$$x_A = P(pro|A) - P(con|A) \qquad (1)$$

$P(S|A)$, in which S denotes either the pro or con standpoint, is the probability that an opinion randomly selected from a set of opinions addressing

[2]http://moviessearch.yahoo.co.jp/detail?ty=mv&id=321602

[3]http://chasen.naist.jp/hiki/ChaSen/

[4]http://cl.aist-nara.ac.jp/~taku-ku/software/cabocha/

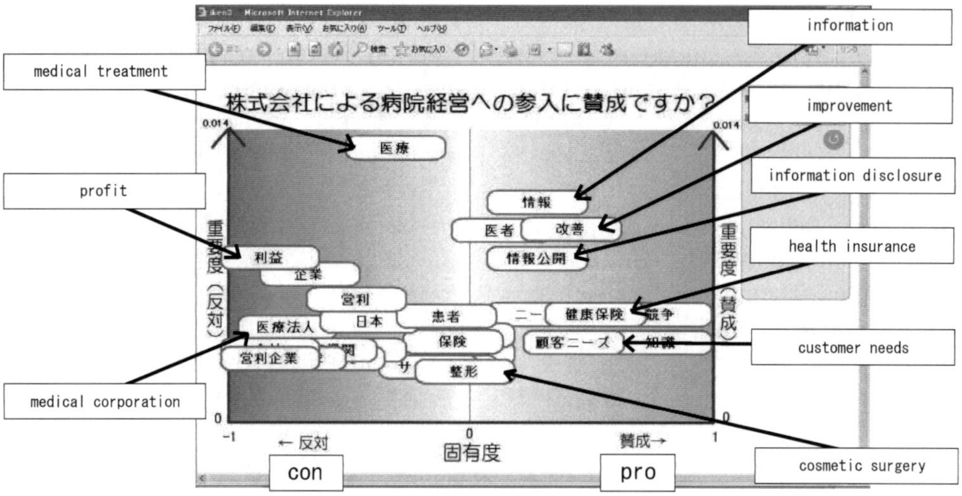

Figure 2: Example of visualizing points at issue for “privatization of hospitals by joint-stock companies”.

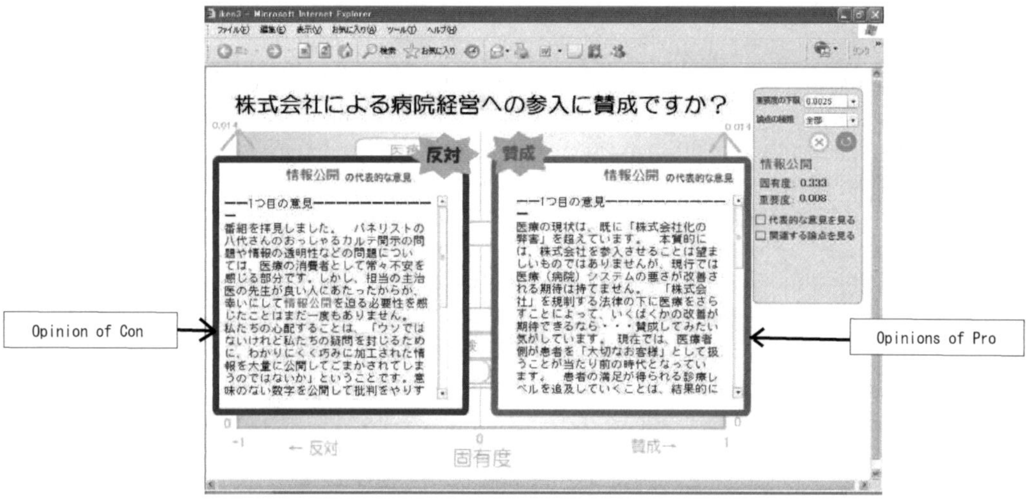

Figure 3: Example of presenting representative opinions for “information disclosure”.

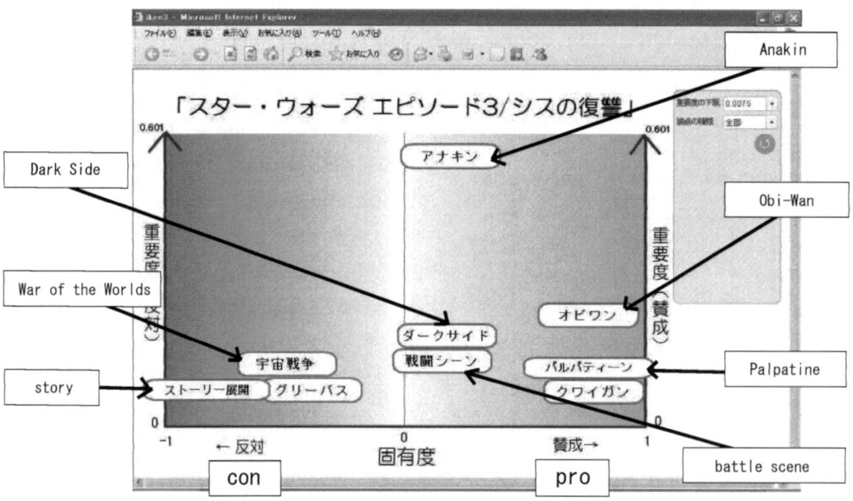

Figure 4: Example of summarizing reviews with multipoint scale rating for “Star Wars: Episode III”.

A supports S. We calculate $P(S|A)$ as the number of opinions that are classified into S and that include A, divided by the number of opinions that include A.

x_A ranges from -1 to 1. A is classified into one of the following three categories depending on the value of x_A:

- if A appears in the pros more frequently than in the cons, x_A is a positive number,
- if A appears in the pros and cons equally often, x_A is zero,
- if A appears in the cons more frequently than in the pros, x_A is a negative number.

The calculation of the y-coordinate of A, y_A depends on which of the above categories applies to A. If A appears in standpoint S more frequently than in its opposite, we define y_A as the probability that a point at issue randomly selected from the opinions classified into S is A.

We calculate y_A as the frequency of A in the opinions classified into S, divided by the total frequencies of points at issue in the opinions classified into S. Thus, y_A ranges from 0 to 1.

However, if A appears in the pros and cons equally often, we use the average of the values of y_A for both standpoints.

General words, which are usually high frequency words, tend to have high values for y_A. Therefore, we discard the words whose y_A is above a predefined threshold. We empirically set the threshold at 0.02.

Table 1 shows example points at issue for the topic "privatization of hospitals by joint-stock companies" and their values of x_A and y_A. In Table 1, points at issue, which have been translated into English, are classified into the three categories (i.e., pro, neutral, and con) according to x_A and are sorted according to y_A in descending order, for each category.

In Table 1, "improvement" is the most important in the pro category, and "medical corporation" is the most important in the con category. In the pro category, many people expect that the quality of medical treatment will be improved if joint-stock companies make inroads into the medical industry. However, in the con category, many people are concerned about the future of existing medical corporations.

Table 1: Examples of points at issue and their coordinates for "privatization of hospitals by joint-stock companies".

Point at issue	x_A	y_A
improvement	0.33	9.2×10^{-3}
information disclosure	0.33	7.9×10^{-3}
health insurance	0.60	5.3×10^{-3}
customer needs	0.50	3.9×10^{-3}
cosmetic surgery	0.00	2.6×10^{-3}
medical corporation	-0.69	4.4×10^{-3}
medical institution	-0.64	3.6×10^{-3}
medical cost	-0.60	3.2×10^{-3}
profit seeking	-0.78	3.2×10^{-3}

4.3 Ranking Opinions

Given a set of opinions from which a point at issue has been extracted, our purpose now is to rank the opinions in order of importance. We assume that representative opinions contain many content words that occur frequently in the opinion set. In our case, content words are nouns, verbs, and adjectives identified by morphological analysis.

We calculate the score of a content word w, $s(w)$, as the frequency of w in the opinion set. We calculate the importance of an opinion by the sum of $s(w)$ for the words in the opinion. However, we normalize the importance of the opinion by the number of words in the opinion because long opinions usually include many words.

5 Experiments

5.1 Method

The effectiveness of our system should be evaluated from different perspectives. First, the effectiveness of each component of our system should be evaluated. Second, the effectiveness of the system as a whole should be evaluated. In this second evaluation, the evaluation measure is the extent to which the decisions of users can be made correctly and efficiently.

As a first step in our research, in this paper we perform only the first evaluation and evaluate the effectiveness of the methods described in Section 4. We used the following Japanese websites as the source of opinions, in which pros and cons are posted for specific topics.

(a) BS debate[5]
(b) ewoman[6]

[5]http://www.nhk.or.jp/bsdebate/
[6]http://www.ewoman.co.jp/

(c) Official website of the prime minister of Japan and his cabinet[7]

(d) Yomiuri online[8]

For evaluation purposes, we collected the pros and cons for five topics. Table 2 shows the five topics, the number of opinions, and the sources. For topic #4, we used the opinions collected from two sources to increase the number of opinions.

In Table 2, the background of topic #5 should perhaps be explained. When using escalators, it is often customary for passengers to stand on one side (either left or right) to allow other passengers to walk past them. However, some people insist that walking on escalators, which are moving stairs, is dangerous.

Graduate students, none of who was an author of this paper, served as assessors, and produced reference data. The output of a method under evaluation was compared with the reference data.

For each topic, two assessors were assigned to enhance the degree of objectivity of the results. Final results were obtained by averaging the results over the assessors and the topics.

5.2 Evaluation of Extracting Points at Issue

For each topic used in the experiments, the assessors read the opinions from both standpoints and extracted the points at issue. We defined the point at issue as the grounds for an argument. We did not restrict the form of the points at issue. Thus, the assessors were allowed to extract any continuous language units, such as words, phrases, sentences, and paragraphs, as points at issue.

Because our method is intended to extract points at issue exhaustively and accurately, we used recall and precision as evaluation measures for the extraction.

Recall is the ratio of the number of correct answers extracted automatically to the total number of correct answers. Precision is the ratio of the number of correct answers extracted automatically to the total number of points at issue extracted automatically.

Table 3 shows the results for each topic, in which "System" denotes the number of points at issue extracted automatically. In Table 3, "C", "R", and "P" denote the number of correct answers, recall, and precision, respectively, on an assessor-by-assessor basis.

[7] http://www.kantei.go.jp/

[8] http://www.yomiuri.co.jp/komachi/forum/

Looking at Table 3, we see that the results can vary depending on the topic and the assessor. However, recall and precision were approximately 50% and 4%, respectively, on average.

The ratio of agreement between assessors was low. When we used the points at issue extracted by one assessor as correct answers and evaluated the effectiveness of the other assessor in the extraction, the recall and precision ranged from 10% to 20% depending on the topic. To increase the ratio of agreement between assessors, the instruction for assessors needs to be revised for future work.

This was mainly because the viewpoint for a target topic and the language units to be extracted were different, depending on the assessor. Because our automatic method extracted points at issue exhaustively, the recall was high and the precision was low, irrespective of the assessor.

The ratios of noun phrases (including nouns) and verb phrases to the number of manually extracted points at issue were 78.5% and 2.0%, respectively. Although the ratio for verb phrases is relatively low, extracting both noun and verb phrases is meaningful.

The recalls of our method for noun phrases and verb phrases were 60.0% and 44.3%, respectively. Errors were mainly due to noun phrases that were not modeled in our method, such as noun phrases that include a relative clause.

5.3 Evaluation of Arranging Points at Issue

As explained in Section 4.2, in our system the points at issue are arranged in a two-dimensional space. The x and y axes correspond to the polarity and the importance of points at issue, respectively.

Because it is difficult for the assessors to judge the correctness of coordinate values in the two-dimensional space, we evaluated the effectiveness of arranging points at issue indirectly.

First, we evaluated the effectiveness of the calculation for the y-axis. We sorted the points at issue, which were extracted automatically (see Section 5.2), according to their importance. We evaluated the trade-off between recall and precision by varying the threshold of y_A. We discarded the points at issue whose y_A is below the threshold.

Note that while this threshold was used to determine the lower bound of y_A, the threshold explained in Section 4.2 (i.e., 0.02) was used to determine the upper bound of y_A and was used consistently irrespective of the lower bound threshold.

Table 2: Topics used for experiments.

Topic ID	Topic	#Opinions Pro	#Opinions Con	Source
#1	principle of result in private companies	57	29	(a)
#2	privatization of hospitals by joint-stock companies	27	44	(a)
#3	the summertime system in Japan	14	17	(b)
#4	privatization of postal services	28	20	(b), (c)
#5	one side walk on an escalator	29	42	(d)

Table 3: Recall and precision of extracting points at issue (C: # of correct answers, R: recall (%), P: precision (%)).

		Assessor A			Assessor B		
Topic ID	System	C	R	P	C	R	P
#1	1968	194	58.2	5.7	101	44.6	2.3
#2	1864	66	50.0	1.8	194	60.8	6.3
#3	508	43	48.8	4.1	43	60.5	5.1
#4	949	77	64.9	5.3	96	36.5	3.7
#5	711	91	30.0	3.8	75	18.7	2.0

Table 4 shows the results, in which the precision was improved to 50% by increasing the threshold. In Figure 2, users can change the threshold of importance by using the panel on the right side to control the number of points at issue presented in the interface. As a result, users can choose appropriate points at issue precisely.

Second, we evaluated the effectiveness of the calculation for the x-axis. We evaluated the effectiveness of our method in a binary classification. For each point at issue extracted by an assessor, the assessor judged which of the two standpoints the point supports.

If a point at issue whose x-coordinate calculated by our method is positive (or negative), it was classified as pro (or con) automatically. We did not use the points at issue whose x-coordinate was zero for evaluation purposes.

Table 5 shows the results. While the number of target points at issue was different depending on the topic and the assessor, the difference in classification accuracy was marginal.

For each topic, we averaged the accuracy determined by each assessor and averaged the accuracies over the topic, which gave 95.6%. Overall, our method performs the binary classification for points at issue with a high accuracy.

Errors were mainly due to opinions that included arguments for both standpoints. For example, a person supporting a standpoint might suggest that he/she would support the other side under a specific condition. Points at issue classified incorrectly had usually been extracted from such contradictory opinions.

5.4 Evaluation of Ranking Opinions

To evaluate the effectiveness of our method in ranking opinions on a point-by-point basis, we used a method that sorts the opinions randomly as a control. We compared the accuracy of our method and that of the control. The accuracy is the ratio of the number of correct answers to the number of opinions presented by the method under evaluation.

For each point at issue extracted by an assessor, the assessor assigned the opinions to one of the following degrees:

- A: the opinion argues about the point at issue and is represented,
- B: the opinion argues about the point at issue but is not represented,
- C: the opinion includes the point at issue but does not argue about it.

We varied the number of top opinions presented by changing the threshold for the rank of opinions.

Table 6 shows the results, in which N denotes the number of top opinions presented. The column "Answer" refers to two cases: the case in which only the opinions assigned to "A" were regarded as correct answers, and the case in which the opinions assigned to "A" or "B" were regarded as correct answers. In either case, our method outperformed the control in ranking accuracy.

Although the accuracy of our method for "A" opinions was low, the accuracy for "A" and "B"

Table 4: Trade-off between recall and precision in extracting points at issue.

Threshold	0	0.002	0.004	0.006	0.008	0.010
Recall	0.48	0.17	0.11	0.04	0.03	0.02
Precision	0.04	0.14	0.21	0.31	0.33	0.50

Table 5: Accuracy for classifying points at issue.

	Assessor A		Assessor B	
Topic ID	#Points	Accuracy (%)	#Points	Accuracy (%)
#1	113	98.2	45	97.7
#2	33	91.0	118	94.1
#3	21	95.2	26	100
#4	50	92.0	35	91.4
#5	27	96.3	14	100

Table 6: Accuracy of ranking opinions.

Answer	Method	$N = 1$	$N = 2$	$N = 3$
A	Random	19%	28%	19%
	Ours	38%	32%	23%
A+B	Random	81%	83%	75%
	Ours	87%	87%	83%

opinions was high. This suggests that our method is effective in distinguishing opinions that argue about a specific point and opinions that include the point but do not argue about it.

6 Conclusion

In aiming to support users' decision making, we have proposed a method for summarizing and visualizing the pro and con arguments about a topic.

Our prototype system, called "OpinionReader", extracts points at issue from the opinions for both pro and con standpoints, arranges the points in a two-dimensional space, and allows users to read important opinions on a point-by-point basis. We have experimentally evaluated the effectiveness of the components of our system.

Future work will include evaluating our system as a whole, and summarizing opinions that change over time.

References

Philip Beineke, Trevor Hastie, and Shivakumar Vaithyanathan. 2004. The sentimental factor: Improving review classification via human-provided information. In *Proceedings of the 42nd Annual Meeting of the Association for Computational Linguistics*, pages 264–271.

Kushal Dave, Steve Lawrence, and David M. Pennock. 2003. Mining the peanut gallery: Opinion extraction and semantic classification of product reviews. In *Proceedings of the 12th International World Wide Web Conference*.

Minqing Hu and Bing Liu. 2004. Mining and summarizing customer reviews. In *Proceedings of the Tenth ACM SIGKDD International Conference on Knowledge Discovery and Data Mining*, pages 168–177.

Soo-Min Kim and Eduard Hovy. 2004. Determining the sentiment of opinions. In *Proceedings of the 20th International Conference on Computational Linguistics*, pages 1367–1373.

Lun-Wei Ku, Li-Ying Lee, Tung-Ho Wu, and Hsin-Hsi Chen. 2005. Major topic detection and its application to opinion summarization. In *Proceedings of the 28th Annual International ACM SIGIR Conference on Research and Development in Information Retrieval*, pages 627–628.

Bing Liu, Minqing Hu, and Junsheng Cheng. 2005. Opinion observer: Analyzing and comparing opinions on the Web. In *Proceedings of the 14th International World Wide Web Conference*, pages 324–351.

Tomoyuki Nanno, Toshiaki Fujiki, Yasuhiro Suzuki, and Manabu Okumura. 2004. Automatically collecting, monitoring, and mining Japanese weblogs. In *The 13th International World Wide Web Conference*, pages 320–321. (poster session).

Bo Pang and Lillian Lee. 2004. A sentimental education: Sentiment analysis using subjectivity summarization based on minimum cuts. In *Proceedings of the 42nd Annual Meeting of the Association for Computational Linguistics*, pages 264–271.

Bo Pang and Lillian Lee. 2005. Seeing stars: Exploiting class relationships for sentiment categorization with respect to rating scales. In *Proceedings of the 43rd Annual Meeting of the Association for Computational Linguistics*, pages 115–124.

Ellen Riloff and Janyce Wiebe. 2003. Learning extraction patterns for subjective expressions. In *Proceedings of the 2003 Conference on Empirical Methods in Natural Language Processing*, pages 105–112.

User-directed Sentiment Analysis: Visualizing the Affective Content of Documents

Michelle L. Gregory
PNNL
902 Battelle Blvd.
Richland Wa. 99354
michelle.gregory@pnl.gov

Nancy Chinchor
Consultant
chinchor@earthlink.net

Paul Whitney
PNNL
902 Battelle Blvd.
Richland Wa. 99354
paul.whitney@pnl.gov

Richard Carter
PNNL
902 Battelle Blvd.
Richland Wa. 99354
richard.carter@pnl.gov

Elizabeth Hetzler
PNNL
902 Battelle Blvd.
Richland Wa. 99354
beth.hetzler@pnl.gov

Alan Turner
PNNL
902 Battelle Blvd.
Richland Wa. 99354
alan.turner@pnl.gov

Abstract

Recent advances in text analysis have led to finer-grained semantic analysis, including *automatic sentiment analysis*—the task of measuring documents, or chunks of text, based on emotive categories, such as *positive* or *negative*. However, considerably less progress has been made on efficient ways of exploring these measurements. This paper discusses approaches for visualizing the affective content of documents and describes an interactive capability for exploring emotion in a large document collection.

1 Introduction

Recent advances in text analysis have led to finer-grained semantic classification, which enables the automatic exploration of subtle areas of meaning. One area that has received a lot of attention is *automatic sentiment analysis*—the task of classifying documents, or chunks of text, into emotive categories, such as *positive* or *negative*. Sentiment analysis is generally used for tracking people's attitudes about particular individuals or items. For example, corporations use sentiment analysis to determine employee attitude and customer satisfaction with their products. Given the plethora of data in digital form, the ability to accurately and efficiently measure the emotional content of documents is paramount.

The focus of much of the automatic sentiment analysis research is on identifying the *affect bearing* words (words with emotional content) and on measurement approaches for sentiment (Turney & Littman, 2003; Pang & Lee, 2004; Wilson et al., 2005). While identifying related content is an essential component for automatic sentiment analysis, it only provides half the story. A useful area of research that has received much less attention is how these measurements might be presented to the users for exploration and added value.

This paper discusses approaches for visualizing affect and describes an interactive capability for exploring emotion in a large document collection. In Section 2 we review current approaches to identifying the affective content of documents, as well as possible ways of visualizing it. In Section 3 we describe our approach: The combination of a lexical scoring method to determine the affective content of documents and a visual analytics tool for visualizing it. We provide a detailed case study in Section 4, followed by a discussion of possible evaluations.

2 Background

At the AAAI Symposium on Attitude and Affect held at Stanford in 2004 (Qu et al., 2005), it was clear that the lexical approach to capturing affect was adequate for broad brush results, but there were no production quality visualizations for presenting those results analytically. Thus, we began exploring methods and tools for the visualization of lexically-based approaches for measuring affect which could facilitate the exploration of affect within a text collection.

2.1 Affect Extraction

Following the general methodology of informational retrieval, there are two pre-dominant methods for identifying sentiment in text: Text classification models and lexical approaches. Classification models require that a set of documents are hand labeled for affect, and a system is

Proceedings of the Workshop on Sentiment and Subjectivity in Text, pages 23–30,
Sydney, July 2006.

trained on the feature vectors associated with labels. New text is automatically classified by comparing the feature vectors with the training set. (Pang & Lee, 2004; Aue & Gamon, 2005). This methodology generally requires a large amount of training data and is domain dependent.

In the lexical approach, documents (Turney & Littman, 2003), phrases (see Wilson et al., 2005), or sentences (Weibe & Riloff, 2005) are categorized as *positive* or *negative*, for example, based on the number of words in them that match a lexicon of sentiment bearing terms. Major drawbacks of this approach include the contextual variability of sentiment (what is *positive* in one domain may not be in another) and incomplete coverage of the lexicon. This latter drawback is often circumvented by employing *bootstrapping* (Turney & Littman, 2003; Weibe & Riloff, 2005) which allows one to create a larger lexicon from a small number of seed words, and potentially one specific to a particular domain.

2.2 Affect Visualization

The uses of automatic sentiment classification are clear (public opinion, customer reviews, product analysis, etc.). However, there has not been a great deal of research into ways of visualizing affective content in ways that might aid data exploration and the analytic process.

There are a number of visualizations designed to reveal the emotional content of text, in particular, text that is thought to be highly emotively charged such as conversational transcripts and chat room transcripts (see DiMicco et al., 2002; Tat & Carpendale, 2002; Lieberman et al., 2004; Wang et al., 2004, for example). Aside from using color and emoticons to explore individual documents (Liu et al., 2003) or email inboxes (Mandic & Kerne, 2004), there are very few visualizations suitable for exploring the affect of large collections of text. One exception is the work of Liu et al. (2005) in which they provide a visualization tool to compare reviews of products,using a bar graph metaphor. Their system automatically extracts product features (with associated affect) through parsing and pos tagging, having to handle exceptional cases individually. Their Opinion Observer is a powerful tool designed for a single purpose: comparing customer reviews.

In this paper, we introduce a visual analytic tool designed to explore the emotional content of large collections of open domain documents. The tools described here work with document collections of all sizes, structures (html, xml, .doc, email, etc), sources (private collections, web, etc.), and types of document collections. The visualization tool is a mature tool that supports the analytical process by enabling users to explore the thematic content of the collection, use natural language to query the collection, make groups, view documents by time, etc. The ability to explore the emotional content of an entire collection of documents not only enables users to compare the range of affect in documents within the collection, but also allows them to relate affect to other dimensions in the collection, such as major topics and themes, time, and source.

3 The Approach

Our methodology combines a traditional lexical approach to scoring documents for affect with a mature visualization tool. We first automatically identify affect by comparing each document against a lexicon of affect-bearing words and obtain an affect score for each document. We provide a number of visual metaphors to represent the affect in the collection and a number of tools that can be used to interactively explore the affective content of the data.

3.1 Lexicon and Measurement

We use a lexicon of affect-bearing words to identify the distribution of affect in the documents. Our lexicon authoring system allows affect-bearing terms, and their associated strengths, to be bulk loaded, declared manually, or algorithmically suggested. In this paper, we use a lexicon derived from the General Inquirer (GI) and supplemented with lexical items derived from a semi-supervised bootstrapping task. The GI tool is a computer-assisted approach for content analyses of textual data (Stone, 1977). It includes an extensive lexicon of over 11,000 hand-coded word stems and 182 categories.

We used this lexicon, specifically the *positive* and *negative* axes, to create a larger lexicon by bootstrapping. Lexical bootstrapping is a method used to help expand dictionaries of semantic categories (Riloff & Jones, 1999) in the context of a document set of interest. The approach we have adopted begins with a lexicon of affect bearing words (POS and NEG) and a corpus. Each document in the corpus receives an affect score by counting the number of words from the seed lexicon that occur in the document; a separate score is given for each affect axis. Words in the corpus are scored for affect potential by comparing their distribution (using an L1 Distribution metric) of occurrence over the set if documents to the distribution of affect bearing words. Words that compare favorably with affect are hypothesized as affect bearing words. Results are then manually culled to determine if in fact they should be included in the lexicon.

Here we report on results using a lexicon built from 8 affect categories, comprising 4 concept pairs:

- Positive (*n*=2236)-Negative (*n*=2708)
- Virtue (*n*=638)-Vice (*n*=649)
- Pleasure (*n*=151)-Pain (*n*=220)
- Power Cooperative (*n*=103)-Power Conflict (*n*=194)

Each document in the collection is compared against all 8 affect categories and receives a score for each. Scores are based on the summation of each affect axis in the document, normalized by the number of words in the documents. This provides an overall proportion of *positive* words, for example, per document. Scores can also be calculated as the summation of each axis, normalized by the total number of affect words for all axes. This allows one to quickly estimate the balance of affect in the documents. For example, using this measurement, one could see that a particular document contains as many *positive* as *negative* terms, or if it is heavily skewed towards one or the other.

While the results reported here are based on a predefined lexicon, our system does include a *Lexicon Editor* in which a user can manually enter their own lexicon or add strengths to lexical items. Included in the editor is a *Lexicon Bootstrapping Utility* which the user can use to help create a specialized lexicon of their own. This utility runs as described above. Note that while we enable the capability of strength, we have not experimented with that variable here. All words for all axes have a default strength of .5.

3.2 Visualization

To visualize the affective content of a collection of documents, we combined a variety of visual metaphors with a tool designed for visual analytics of documents, IN-SPIRE.

3.2.1 The IN-SPIRE System

IN-SPIRE (Hetzler and Turner, 2004) is a visual analytics tool designed to facilitate rapid understanding of large textual corpora. IN-SPIRE generates a compiled document set from *mathematical signatures* for each document in a set. Document signatures are clustered according to common themes to enable information exploration and visualizations. Information is presented to the user using several *visual metaphors* to expose different facets of the textual data. The central visual metaphor is a **Galaxy view** of the corpus that allows users to intuitively interact with thousands of documents, examining them by theme (see Figure 4, below). IN-SPIRE leverages the use of context vectors such as LSA (Deerwester et al., 1990) for document clustering and projection. Additional analytic tools allow exploration of temporal trends, thematic distribution by source or other metadata, and query relationships and overlaps. IN-SPIRE was recently enhanced to support visual analysis of sentiment.

3.2.2 Visual Metaphors

In selecting metaphors to represent the affect scores of documents, we started by identifying the kinds of questions that users would want to explore. Consider, as a guiding example, a set of customer reviews for several commercial products (Hu & Liu, 2004). A user reviewing this data might be interested in a number of questions, such as:

- What is the range of affect overall?
- Which products are viewed most positively? Most negatively?
- What is the range of affect for a particular product?
- How does the affect in the reviews deviate from the norm? Which are more negative or positive than would be expected from the averages?
- How does the feedback of one product compare to that of another?
- Can we isolate the affect as it pertains to different features of the products?

In selecting a base metaphor for affect, we wanted to be able to address these kinds of questions. We wanted a metaphor that would support viewing affect axes individually as well as in pairs. In addition to representing the most common axes, negative and positive, we wanted to provide more flexibility by incorporating the ability to portray multiple pairs because we suspect that additional axes will help the user explore nuances of emotion in the data. For our current metaphor, we drew inspiration from the Rose plot used by Florence Nightingale (Wainer, 1997). This metaphor is appealing in that it is easily interpreted, that larger scores draw more attention, and that measures are shown in consistent relative location, making it easier to compare measures across document groups. We use a modified version of this metaphor in which each axis is represented individually but is also paired with its opposite to aid in direct comparisons. To this end, we vary the spacing between the rose petals to reinforce the pairing. We also use color; each pair has a common hue, with the more positive of the pair shown in a lighter shade and the more negative one in a darker shade (see Figure 1).

To address how much the range of affect varies across a set of documents, we adapted the concept of a box plot to the rose petal. For each axis, we show the median and quartile values as shown in the figure below. The dark line indicates the median value and the color band portrays the quartiles. In the plot in Figure 1, for example, the scores vary quite a bit.

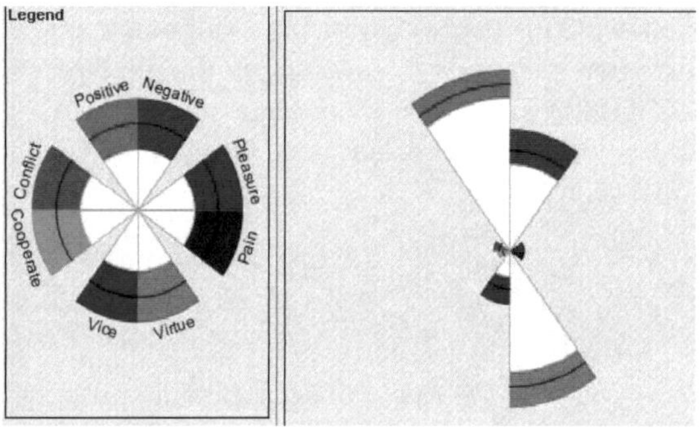

Figure 1. Rose plot adapted to show median and quartile variation.

Another variation we made on the base metaphor was to address a more subtle set of questions. It may happen that the affect scores within a dataset are largely driven by document membership in particular groups. For example, in our customer data, it may be that all documents about Product A are relatively positive while those about Product B are relatively negative. A user wanting to understand customer complaints may have a subtle need. It is not sufficient to just look at the most negative documents in the dataset, because none of the Product A documents may pass this threshold. What may also help is to look at all documents that are more negative than one would expect, given the product they discuss. To carry out this calculation, we use a statistical technique to calculate the Main (or expected) affect value for each group and the Residual (or deviation) affect value for each document with respect to its group (Scheffe, 1999).

To convey the Residual concept, we needed a representation of deviation from expected value. We also wanted this portrayal to be similar to the base metaphor. We use a unit circle to portray the expected value and show deviation by drawing the appropriate rose petals either outside (larger than expected) or inside (smaller than expected) the unit circle, with the color amount showing the amount of deviation from expected. In the figures below, the dotted circle represents expected value. The glyph on the left shows a cluster with scores slightly higher than expected for Positive and for Cooperation affect. The glyph on the right shows a cluster with scores slightly higher than expected for the Negative and Vice affect axes (Figure 2).

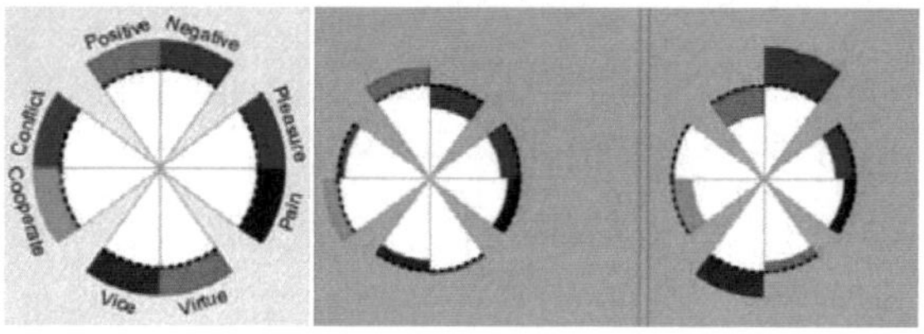

Figure 2. Rose plot adapted to show deviation from expected values.

3.2.3 Visual Interaction

IN-SPIRE includes a variety of analytic tools that allow exploration of temporal trends, thematic distribution by source or other metadata, and query relationships and overlaps. We have incorporated several interaction capabilities for further exploration of the affect. Our analysis system allows users to group documents in numerous ways, such as by query results, by metadata (such as the product), by time frame, and by similarity in themes. A user can select one or more of these groups and see a summary of affect and its variation in those groups. In addition, the group members are clustered by their affect scores and glyphs of the residual, or variation from expected value, are shown for each of these sub-group clusters.

Below each rose we display a small histogram showing the number of documents represented by that glyph (see Figure 3). These allow comparison of affect to cluster or group size. For example, we find that extreme affect scores are typically found in the smaller clusters, while larger ones often show more mid-range scores. As the user selects document groups or clusters, we show the proportion of documents selected.

Figure 3. Clusters by affect score, with one rose plot per cluster.

The interaction may also be driven from the affect size. If a given clustering of affect characteristics is selected, the user can see the themes they represent, how they correlate to metadata, or the time distribution. We illustrate how the affect visualization and interaction fit into a larger analysis with a brief case study.

4 Case study

The IN-SPIRE visualization tool is a non-data specific tool, designed to explore large amounts of textual data for a variety of genres and document types (doc, xml, etc). Many users of the system have their own data sets they wish to explore (company internal documents), or data can be harvested directly from the web, either in a single web harvest, or dynamically. The case study and dataset presented here is intended as an example only, it does not represent the full range of exploration capabilities of the affective content of datasets.

We explore a set of customer reviews, comprising a collection of Amazon reviews for five products (Hu & Liu, 2004). While a customer may not want to explore reviews for 5 different product types at once, the dataset is realistic in that a web harvest of one review site will contain reviews of multiple products. This allows us to demonstrate how the tool enables users to focus on the data and comparisons that they are interested in exploring. The 5 products in this dataset are:

- Canon G3; digital camera
- Nikon coolpix 4300; digital camera
- Nokia 6610; cell phone
- Creative Labs Nomad Jukebox Zen Xtra 40GB; mp3 player
- Apex AD2600 Progressive-scan DVD player

We begin by clustering the reviews, based on overall thematic content. The labels are automatically generated and indicate some of the stronger theme combinations in this dataset. These clusters are driven largely by product vocabulary. The two cameras cluster in the lower portion; the Zen shows up in the upper right clusters, with the phone in the middle and the Apex DVD player in the upper left and upper middle. In this image, the pink dots are the Apex DVD reviews.

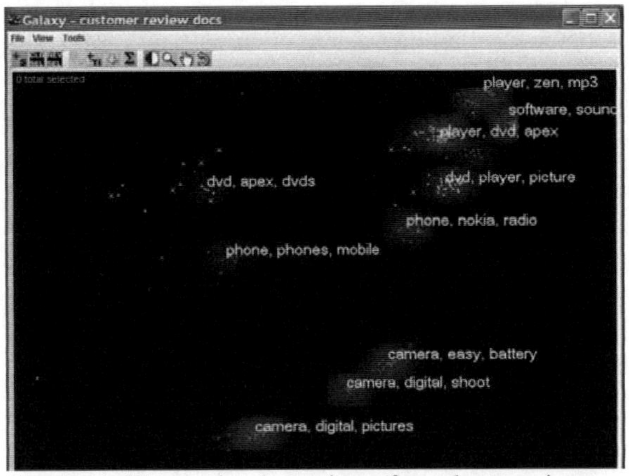

Figure 4. Thematic clustering of product review

The affect measurements on these documents generate five clusters in our system, each of which is summarized with a rose plot showing affect variation. This gives us information on the range and distribution of affect overall in this data. We can select one of these plots, either to review the documents or to interact further. Selection is indicated with a green border, as shown in the upper middle plot of Figure 5.

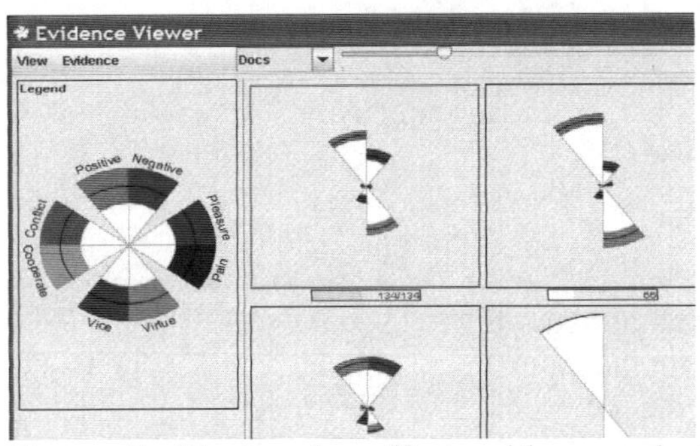

Figure 5. Clusters by affect, with one cluster glyph selected.

The selected documents are relatively positive; they have higher scores in the Positive and Virtue axes and lower scores in the Negative axis. We may want to see how the documents in this affect cluster distribute over the five products. This question is answered by the correlation tool, shown in Figure 6; the positive affect cluster contains more reviews on the Zen MP3 player than any of the other products.

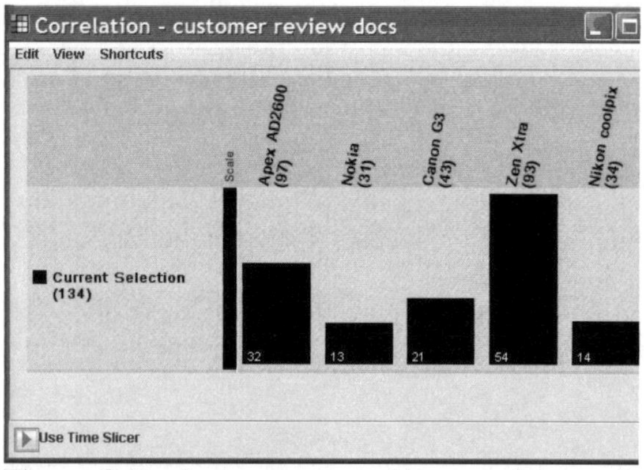

Figure 6. Products represented in one of the positive affect clusters.

Alternatively we could get a summary of affect per product. Figure 7 shows the affect for the Apex DVD player and the Nokia cell phone. While both are positive, the Apex has stronger negative ratings than the Nokia.

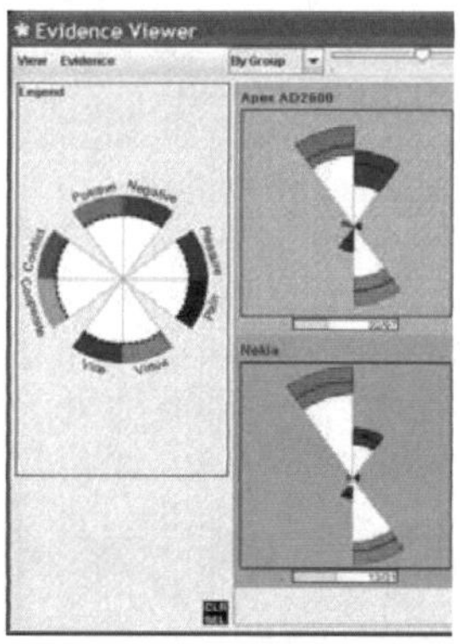

Figure 7. Comparison of Affect Scores of Nokia to Apex

More detail is apparent by looking at the clusters within one or more groups and examining the deviations. Figure 8 shows the sub-clusters within the Apex group. We include the summary for the group as a whole (directly beneath the Apex label), and then show the four sub-clusters by illustrating how they deviate from expected value. We see that two of these tend to be more positive than expected and two are more negative than expected.

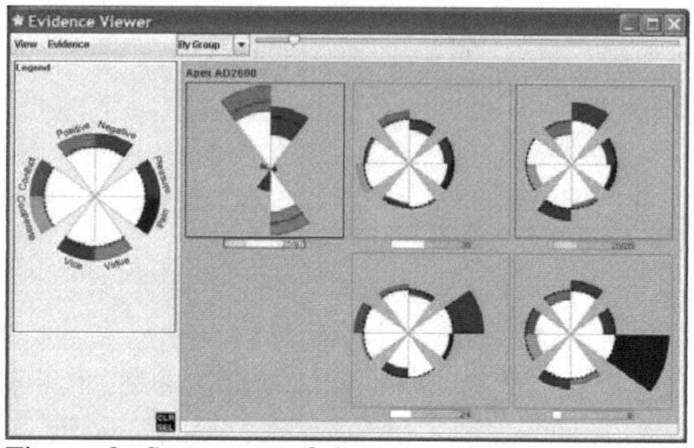

Figure 8. Summary of Apex products with sub-clusters showing deviations.

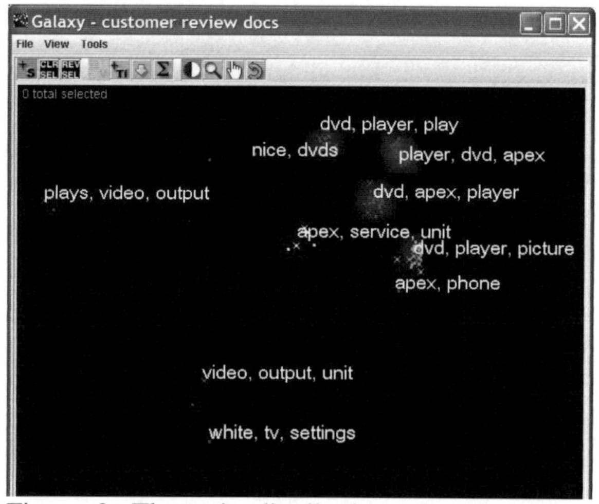

Figure 9. Thematic distribution of reviews for one product (Apex).

Looking at the thematic distribution among the Apex documents shows topics that dominate its reviews (Figure 9).

We can examine the affect across these various clusters. Figure 10 shows the comparison of the "service" cluster to the "dvd player picture" cluster. This graphic demonstrates that documents with "service" as a main theme tend to be much more negative, while documents with "picture" as a main theme are much more positive.

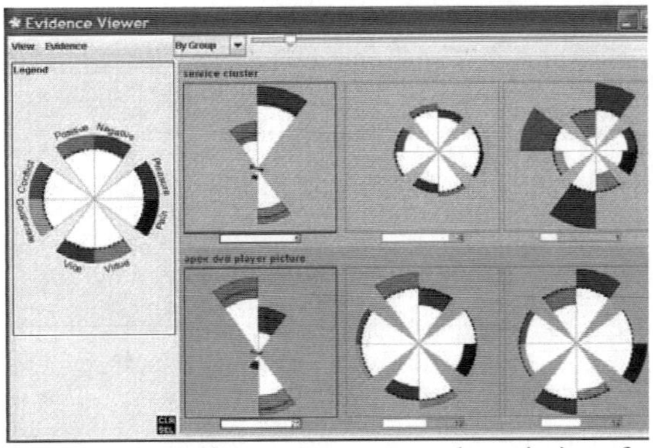

Figure 10. Affect summary and variation for "service" cluster and "picture" cluster.

The visualization tool includes a document viewer so that any selection of documents can be reviewed. For example, a user may be interested in why the "service" documents tend to be negative, in which case they can review the original reviews. The doc viewer, shown in Figure 11, can be used at any stage in the process with any number of documents selected. Individual documents can be viewed by clicking on a document title in the upper portion of the doc viewer.

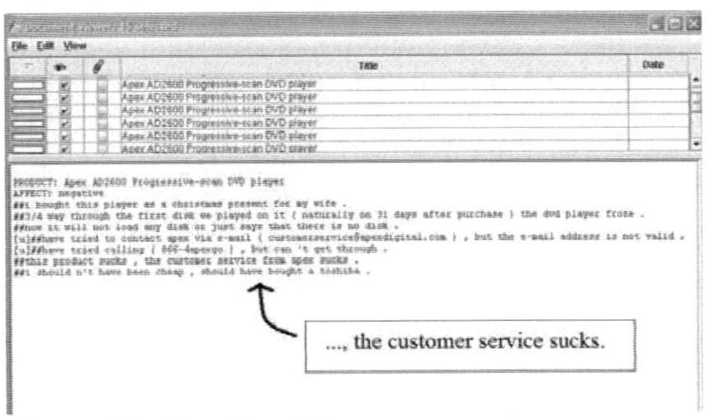

Figure 11: The Doc Viewer.

In this case study, we have illustrated the usefulness of visualizing the emotional content of a document collection. Using the tools presented here, we can summarize the dataset by saying that in general, the customer reviews are positive (Figure 5), but reviews for some products are more positive than others (Figures 6 and 7). In addition to the general content of the reviews, we can narrow our focus to the features contained in the reviews. We saw that while reviews for Apex are generally positive (Figure 8), reviews about Apex "service" tend to be much more negative than reviews about Apex "picture" (Figure 10).

5 Evaluation

IN-SPIRE is a document visualization tool that is designed to explore the thematic content of a large collection of documents. In this paper, we have described the added functionality of exploring affect as one of the possible dimensions. As an exploratory system, it is difficult to define appropriate evaluation metric. Because the goal of our system is not to discretely bin the documents into affect categories, traditional metrics such as precision are not applicable. However, to get a sense of the coverage of our lexicon, we did compare our measurements to the hand annotations provided for the customer review dataset.

The dataset had hand scores (-3-3) for each feature contained in each review. We summed these scores to discretely bin them into positive (>0) or negative (<0). We did this both at the feature level and the review level (by looking at the cumulative score for all the features in the review). We compared these categorizations to the scores output by our measurement tool. If a document had a higher proportion of positive words than negative, we classified it as positive, and negative if it had a higher proportion of negative words. Using a chi-square, we found that the categorizations from our system were related with the hand annotations for both the whole reviews (chi-square=33.02, df=4, $p<0.0001$) and the individual features (chi-square=150.6, df=4, $p<0.0001$), with actual agreement around 71% for both datasets. While this number is not in itself impressive, recall that our lexicon was built independently of the data for which is was applied. W also expect some agreement to be lost by conflating all scores into discrete bins, we expect that if we compared the numeric values of the hand annotations and our scores, we would have stronger correlations.

These scores only provide an indication that the lexicon we used correlates with the hand annotations for the same data. As an exploratory system, however, a better evaluation metric would be a user study in which we get feedback on the usefulness of this capability in accomplishing a variety of analytical tasks. IN-SPIRE is currently deployed in a number of settings, both commercial and government. The added capabilities for interactively exploring affect have recently been deployed. We plan to conduct a variety of user evaluations *in-situ* that focus on its utility in a number of different tasks. Results of these studies will help steer the further development of this methodology.

6 Conclusion

We have developed a measurement and visualization approach to affect that we expect to be useful in the context of the IN-SPIRE text analysis toolkit. Our innovations include the flexibility of the lexicons used, the measurement options, the bootstrapping method and utility for lexicon development, and the visualization of affect using rose plots and interactive exploration in the context of an established text analysis toolkit. While the case study presented here was conducted in English, all tools described are language independent and we have begun exploring and creating lexicons of affect bearing words in multiple languages.

References

A. Aue. & M. Gamon. 2005. Customizing Sentiment Classifiers to New Domains: a Case Study. Submitted RANLP.

S. Deerwester, S.T. Dumais, T.K. Landauer, G.W. Furnas, and R.A. Harshman. 1990. Indexing by Latent Semantic Analysis. *Journal of the Society for Information Science,* 41(6):391–407.

J. M. DiMicco, V. Lakshmipathy, A. T. Fiore. 2002. Conductive Chat: Instant Messaging With a Skin Conductivity Channel. In *Proceedings of Conference on Computer Supported Cooperative Work.*

D. G. Feitelson. 2003. Comparing Partitions with Spie Charts. *Technical Report 2003-87*, School of Computer Science and Engineering, The Hebrew University of Jerusalem.

E. Hetzler and A. Turner. 2004. Analysis Experiences Using Information Visualization. *IEEE Computer Graphics and Applications*, 24(5):22-26, 2004.

M. Hu and B. Liu. 2004. Mining Opinion Features in Customer Reviews. In *Proceedings of Nineteenth National Conference on Artificial Intelligence* (AAAI-2004).

H. Lieberman, H. Liu, P. Singh and B. Barry. 2004. Beating Common Sense into Interactive Applications. *AI Magazine* 25(4): Winter 2004, 63-76.

B. Liu, M. Hu and J. Cheng. 2005. Opinion Observer: Analyzing and Comparing Opinions on the Web. *Proceedings of the 14th international World Wide Web conference (WWW-2005)*, May 10-14, 2005: Chiba, Japan.

H. Liu, T. Selker, H. Lieberman. 2003. Visualizing the Affective Structure of a Text Document. *Computer Human Interaction*, April 5-10, 2003: Fort Lauderdale.

M. Mandic and A. Kerne. 2004. faMailiar—Intimacy-based Email Visualization. In *Proceedings of IEEE Information Visualization 2004*, Austin Texas, 31-32.

B. Pang and L. Lee. 2004. A Sentimental Education: Sentiment Analysis Using Subjectivity Summarization Based on Minimum Cuts. In *Proceedings of the 42nd ACL*, pp. 271-278, 2004.

Y. Qu,, J. Shanahan, and J. Weibe. 2004. Exploring Attitude and Affect in Text: Theories and Applications. Technical Report SS-04-07.

E. Riloff and R. Jones. 1999. Learning Dictionaries for Information Extraction by Multi-Level Bootstrapping. *Proceedings of the Sixteenth National Conference on Artificial Intelligence* (AAAI-99) pp. 474-479.

H. Scheffé. 1999. *The Analysis of Variance*, Wiley-Interscience.

P. Stone. 1977. Thematic Text Analysis: New Agendas for Analyzing Text Content. In *Text Analysis for the Social Sciences*, ed. Carl Roberts, Lawrence Erlbaum Associates.

A. Tat and S. Carpendale. 2002. Visualizing Human Dialog. In *Proceedings of IEEE Conference on Information Visualization*, IV'02, p.16-24, London, UK.

P. Turney and M. Littman. 2003. Measuring Praise and Criticism: Inference of Semantic Orientation from Association. *ACM Transactions on Information Systems* (TOIS) 21:315-346.

H. Wainer. 1997. A Rose by Another Name." *Visual Revelations*, Copernicus Books, New York.

H. Wang, H. Prendinger, and T. Igarashi. 2004. Communicating Emotions in Online Chat Using Physiological Sensors and Animated Text." In *Proceedings of ACM SIGCHI Conference on Human Factors in Computing Systems* (CHI'04), Vienna, Austria, April 24-29.

J. Wiebe and Ellen Riloff. 2005. Creating Subjective and Objective Sentence Classifiers from Unannotated Texts." In *Proceedings of Sixth International Conference on Intelligent Text Processing and Computational Linguistics.*

T. Wilson, J. Wiebe, and P. Hoffmann. 2005. Recognizing Contextual Polarity in Phrase-Level Sentiment Analysis." In *Proceeding of HLT-EMNLP-2005.*

Annotating Attribution in the Penn Discourse TreeBank

Rashmi Prasad and **Nikhil Dinesh** and **Alan Lee** and **Aravind Joshi**
University of Pennsylvania
Philadelphia, PA 19104 USA
{rjprasad,nikhild,aleewk,joshi}@linc.cis.upenn.edu

Bonnie Webber
University of Edinburgh
Edinburgh, EH8 9LW Scotland
bonnie@inf.ed.ac.uk

Abstract

An emerging task in text understanding and generation is to categorize information as fact or opinion and to further attribute it to the appropriate source. Corpus annotation schemes aim to encode such distinctions for NLP applications concerned with such tasks, such as information extraction, question answering, summarization, and generation. We describe an annotation scheme for marking the attribution of abstract objects such as propositions, facts and eventualities associated with discourse relations and their arguments annotated in the Penn Discourse TreeBank. The scheme aims to capture the source and degrees of factuality of the abstract objects. Key aspects of the scheme are annotation of the *text spans* signalling the attribution, and annotation of features recording the *source*, *type*, *scopal polarity*, and *determinacy* of attribution.

1 Introduction

News articles typically contain a mixture of information presented from several different perspectives, and often in complex ways. Writers may present information as known to them, or from some other individual's perspective, while further distinguishing between, for example, whether that perspective involves an assertion or a belief. Recent work has shown the importance of recognizing such perspectivization of information for several NLP applications, such as information extraction, summarization, question answering (Wiebe et al., 2004; Stoyanov et al., 2005; Riloff et al., 2005) and generation (Prasad et al., 2005). Part of the goal of such applications is to distinguish between factual and non-factual information, and to identify the source of the information. Annotation schemes (Wiebe et al., 2005; Wilson and Wiebe, 2005; PDTB-Group, 2006) encode such distinctions to facilitate accurate recognition and representation of such perspectivization of information.

This paper describes an extended annotation scheme for marking the attribution of discourse relations and their arguments annotated in the Penn Discourse TreeBank (PDTB) (Miltsakaki et al., 2004; Prasad et al., 2004; Webber et al., 2005), the primary goal being to capture the source and degrees of factuality of abstract objects. The scheme captures four salient properties of attribution: (a) *source*, distinguishing between different types of agents to whom AOs are attributed, (b) *type*, reflecting the degree of factuality of the AO, (c) *scopal polarity* of attribution, indicating polarity reversals of attributed AOs due to surface negated attributions, and (d) *determinacy* of attribution, indicating the presence of contexts canceling the entailment of attribution. The scheme also describes annotation of the *text spans* signaling the attribution. The proposed scheme is an extension of the core scheme used for annotating attribution in the first release of the PDTB (Dinesh et al., 2005; PDTB-Group, 2006). Section 2 gives an overview of the PDTB, Section 3 presents the extended annotation scheme for attribution, and Section 4 presents the summary.

2 The Penn Discourse TreeBank (PDTB)

The PDTB contains annotations of discourse relations and their arguments on the Wall Street Journal corpus (Marcus et al., 1993). Following the approach towards discourse structure in (Webber et al., 2003), the PDTB takes a lexicalized ap-

Proceedings of the Workshop on Sentiment and Subjectivity in Text, pages 31–38,
Sydney, July 2006. ©2006 Association for Computational Linguistics

proach towards the annotation of discourse relations, treating *discourse connectives* as the anchors of the relations, and thus as discourse-level predicates taking two *abstract objects* (AOs) as their arguments. For example, in (1), the subordinating conjunction *since* is a discourse connective that anchors a TEMPORAL relation between the event of the earthquake hitting and a state where no music is played by a certain woman. (The 4-digit number in parentheses at the end of examples gives the WSJ file number of the example.)

(1) *She hasn't played any music* since **the earthquake hit**. (0766)

There are primarily two types of connectives in the PDTB: "Explicit" and "Implicit". Explicit connectives are identified form four grammatical classes: subordinating conjunctions (e.g., *because, when, only because, particularly since*), subordinators (e.g., *in order that*), coordinating conjunctions (e.g., *and, or*), and discourse adverbials (e.g., *however, otherwise*). In the examples in this paper, Explicit connectives are underlined.

For sentences not related by an Explicit connective, annotators attempt to infer a discourse relation between them by *inserting* connectives (called "Implicit" connectives) that *best* convey the inferred relations. For example, in (2), the inferred CAUSAL relation between the two sentences was annotated with *because* as the Implicit connective. Implicit connectives together with their sense classification are shown here in small caps.

(2) *Also unlike Mr. Ruder, Mr. Breeden appears to be in a position to get somewhere with his agenda.* Implicit=BECAUSE (CAUSE) **As a former White House aide who worked closely with Congress, he is savvy in the ways of Washington.** (0955)

Cases where a suitable Implicit connective could not be annotated between adjacent sentences are annotated as either (a) "EntRel", where the second sentence only serves to provide some further description of an entity in the first sentence (Example 3); (b) "NoRel", where no discourse relation or entity-based relation can be inferred; and (c) "AltLex", where the insertion of an Implicit connective leads to *redundancy*, due to the relation being *alternatively lexicalized* by some "non-connective" expression (Example 4).

(3) *C.B. Rogers Jr. was named chief executive officer of this business information concern.* Implicit=EntRel **Mr. Rogers, 60 years old, succeeds J.V. White, 64, who will remain chairman and chairman of the executive committee (0929)**.

(4) *One in 1981 raised to $2,000 a year from $1,500 the amount a person could put, tax-deductible, into the tax-deferred accounts and widened coverage to people under employer retirement plans.* Implicit=AltLex (consequence) **[This caused] an explosion of IRA promotions by brokers, banks, mutual funds and others**. (0933)

Arguments of connectives are simply labelled Arg2, for the argument appearing in the clause syntactically bound to the connective, and Arg1, for the other argument. In the examples here, Arg1 appears in italics, while Arg2 appears in bold.

The basic unit for the realization of an AO argument of a connective is the clause, tensed or untensed, but it can also be associated with multiple clauses, within or across sentences. *Nominalizations* and *discourse deictics* (*this, that*), which can also be interpreted as AOs, can serve as the argument of a connective too.

The current version of the PDTB also contains attribution annotations on discourse relations and their arguments. These annotations, however, used the earlier core scheme which is subsumed in the extended scheme described in this paper.

The first release of the Penn Discourse TreeBank, PDTB-1.0 (reported in PDTB-Group (2006)), is freely available from `http://www.seas.upenn.edu/~pdtb`. PDTB-1.0 contains 100 distinct types of Explicit connectives, with a total of 18505 tokens, annotated across the entire WSJ corpus (25 sections). Implicit relations have been annotated in three sections (Sections 08, 09, and 10) for the first release, totalling 2003 tokens (1496 Implicit connectives, 19 AltLex relations, 435 EntRel tokens, and 53 NoRel tokens). The corpus also includes a broadly defined sense classification for the implicit relations, and attribution annotation with the earlier core scheme. Subsequent releases of the PDTB will include Implicit relations annotated across the entire corpus, attribution annotation using the extended scheme proposed here, and fine-grained sense classification for both Explicit and Implicit connectives.

3 Annotation of Attribution

Recent work (Wiebe et al., 2005; Prasad et al., 2005; Riloff et al., 2005; Stoyanov et al., 2005), has shown the importance of recognizing and representing the source and factuality of information in certain NLP applications. Information extraction systems, for example, would perform better by prioritizing the presentation of factual information, and multi-perspective question answering systems would benefit from presenting information from different perspectives.

Most of the annotation approaches tackling these issues, however, are aimed at performing classifications at either the document level (Pang et al., 2002; Turney, 2002), or the sentence or word level (Wiebe et al., 2004; Yu and Hatzivassiloglou, 2003). In addition, these approaches focus primarily on sentiment classification, and use the same for getting at the classification of facts vs. opinions. In contrast to these approaches, the focus here is on marking attribution on more analytic semantic units, namely the *Abstract Objects* (AOs) associated with predicate-argument discourse relations annotated in the PDTB, with the aim of providing a compositional classification of the factuality of AOs. The scheme isolates four key properties of attribution, to be annotated as features: (1) *source*, which distinguishes between different types of agents (Section 3.1); (2) *type*, which encodes the nature of relationship between agents and AOs, reflecting the degree of factuality of the AO (Section 3.2); (3) *scopal polarity*, which is marked when surface negated attribution reverses the polarity of the attributed AO (Section 3.3), and (4) *determinacy*, which indicates the presence of contexts due to which the entailment of attribution gets cancelled (Section 3.4). In addition, to further facilitate the task of identifying attribution, the scheme also aims to annotate the *text span* complex signaling attribution (Section 3.5)

Results from annotations using the earlier attribution scheme (PDTB-Group, 2006) show that a significant proportion (34%) of the annotated discourse relations have some non-Writer agent as the source for either the relation or one or both arguments. This illustrates the simplest case of the ambiguity inherent for the factuality of AOs, and shows the potential use of the PDTB annotations towards the automatic classification of factuality. The annotations also show that there are a variety of configurations in which the components of the relations are attributed to different sources, suggesting that recognition of attributions may be a complex task for which an annotated corpus may be useful. For example, in some cases, a relation together with its arguments is attributed to the writer or some other agent, whereas in other cases, while the relation is attributed to the writer, one or both of its arguments is attributed to different agent(s). For Explicit connectives. there were 6 unique configurations, for configurations containing more than 50 tokens, and 5 unique configurations for Implicit connectives.

3.1 Source

The *source* feature distinguishes between (a) the writer of the text ("Wr"), (b) some specific agent introduced in the text ("Ot" for other), and (c) some generic source, i.e., some arbitrary ("Arb") individual(s) indicated via a non-specific reference in the text. The latter two capture further differences in the degree of factuality of AOs with non-writer sources. For example, an "Arb" source for some information conveys a higher degree of factuality than an "Ot" source, since it can be taken to be a "generally accepted" view.

Since arguments can get their attribution through the relation between them, they can be annotated with a fourth value "Inh", to indicate that their source value is inherited from the relation.

Given this scheme for *source*, there are broadly two possibilities. In the first case, a relation and both its arguments are attributed to the same source, either the writer, as in (5), or some other agent (here, Bill Biedermann), as in (6). (Attribution feature values assigned to examples are shown below each example; REL stands for the discourse relation denoted by the connective; Attribution text spans are shown boxed.)

(5) <u>Since</u> **the British auto maker became a takeover target last month**, its ADRs have jumped about 78%. (0048)

	REL	Arg1	Arg2
[Source]	Wr	Inh	Inh

(6) *"The public is buying the market* <u>when</u> **in reality there is plenty of grain to be shipped**," [said Bill Biedermann . . .] (0192)

	REL	Arg1	Arg2
[Source]	Ot	Inh	Inh

As Example (5) shows, text spans for implicit Writer attributions (corresponding to implicit communicative acts such as *I write*, or *I say*), are not marked and are taken to imply Writer attribution by default (see also Section 3.5).

In the second case, one or both arguments have a different source from the relation. In (7), for example, the relation and Arg2 are attributed to the writer, whereas Arg1 is attributed to another agent (here, Mr. Green). On the other hand, in (8) and (9), the relation and Arg1 are attributed to the writer, whereas Arg2 is attributed to another agent.

(7) When **Mr. Green won a $240,000 verdict in a land condemnation case against the state in June 1983,** he says *Judge O'Kicki unexpectedly awarded him an additional $100,000.* (0267)

	REL	Arg1	Arg2
[Source]	Wr	Ot	Inh

(8) *Factory orders and construction outlays were largely flat in December* while purchasing agents said **manufacturing shrank further in October**. (0178)

	REL	Arg1	Arg2
[Source]	Wr	Inh	Ot

(9) *There, on one of his first shopping trips, Mr. Paul picked up several paintings at stunning prices.* ... Afterward, Mr. Paul is said by Mr. Guterman **to have phoned Mr. Guterman, the New York developer selling the collection, and gloated**. (2113)

	REL	Arg1	Arg2
[Source]	Wr	Inh	Ot

Example (10) shows an example of a generic source indicated by an agentless passivized attribution on Arg2 of the relation. Note that passivized attributions can also be associated with a specific source when the agent is explicit, as shown in (9). "Arb" sources are also identified by the occurrences of adverbs like *reportedly, allegedly*, etc.

(10) Although index arbitrage is said **to add liquidity to markets**, John Bachmann, ... says *too much liquidity isn't a good thing.* (0742)

	REL	Arg1	Arg2
[Source]	Wr	Ot	Arb

We conclude this section by noting that "Ot" is used to refer to *any* specific individual as the source. That is, no further annotation is provided to indicate *who* the "Ot" agent in the text is. Furthermore, as shown in Examples (11-12), multiple "Ot" sources within the same relation do not indicate whether or not they refer to the same or different agents. However, we assume that the text span annotations for attribution, together with an independent mechanism for named entity recognition and anaphora resolution can be employed to identify and disambiguate the appropriate references.

(11) *Suppression of the book,* Judge Oakes observed, *would operate as a prior restraint and thus involve the First Amendment.* Moreover, and here Judge Oakes went to the heart of the question, **"Responsible biographers and historians constantly use primary sources, letters, diaries, and memoranda**. (0944)

	REL	Arg1	Arg2
[Source]	Wr	Ot	Ot

(12) *The judge was considered imperious, abrasive and ambitious,* those who practiced before him say. Yet, **despite the judge's imperial bearing, no one ever had reason to suspect possible wrongdoing**, says John Bognato, president of Cambria ... .(0267)

	REL	Arg1	Arg2
[Source]	Wr	Ot	Ot

3.2 Type

The *type* feature signifies the nature of the relation between the agent and the AO, leading to different inferences about the degree of factuality of the AO. In order to capture the factuality of the AOs, we start by making a three-way distinction of AOs into *propositions, facts* and *eventualities* (Asher, 1993). This initial distinction allows for a more semantic, compositional approach to the annotation and recognition of factuality. We define the attribution relations for each AO type as follows: (a) *Propositions* involve attribution to an agent of his/her (varying degrees of) commitment towards the truth of a proposition; (b) *Facts* involve attribution to an agent of an evaluation towards or knowledge of a proposition whose truth is taken for granted (i.e., a presupposed proposition); and (c) *Eventualities* involve attribution to an agent of an intention/attitude towards an eventuality. In the case of *propositions*, a further distinction is made to capture the difference in the degree of the agent's commitment towards the truth of the proposition, by distinguishing between "assertions" and "beliefs". Thus, the scheme for the annotation of *type* ultimately uses a four-way distinction for AOs, namely between *assertions, beliefs, facts,* and *eventualities.* Initial determination of the degree of factuality involves determination of the type of the AO.

AO types can be identified by well-defined semantic classes of verbs/phrases anchoring the attribution. We consider each of these in turn.

Assertions are identified by "assertive predicates" or "verbs of communication" (Levin, 1993) such as *say, mention, claim, argue, explain* etc. They take the value "Comm" (for verbs of Communication). In Example (13), the Ot attribution on Arg1 takes the value "Comm" for *type*. Implicit writer attributions, as in the relation of (13), also take (the default) "Comm". Note that when an argument's attribution source is not inherited (as in Arg1 in this example) it also takes its own independent value for *type*. This example thus conveys that there are two different attributions expressed within the discourse relation, one for the relation and the other for one of its arguments, and that both involve assertion of propositions.

(13) When **Mr. Green won a $240,000 verdict in a land condemnation case against the state in June 1983**, he says *Judge O'Kicki unexpectedly awarded him an additional $100,000.* (0267)

	REL	Arg1	Arg2
[Source]	Wr	Ot	Inh
[Type]	Comm	Comm	Null

In the absence of an independent occurrence of attribution on an argument, as in Arg2 of Example (13), the "Null" value is used for the *type* on the argument, meaning that it needs to be derived by independent (here, undefined) considerations under the scope of the relation. Note that unlike the "Inh" value of the *source* feature, "Null" does not indicate inheritance. In a subordinate clause, for example, while the relation denoted by the subordinating conjunction may be asserted, the clause content itself may be presupposed, as seems to be the case for the relation and Arg2 of (13). However, we found these differences difficult to determine at times, and consequently leave this undefined in the current scheme.

Beliefs are identified by "propositional attitude verbs" (Hintikka, 1971) such as *believe*, *think*, *expect*, *suppose*, *imagine*, etc. They take the value "PAtt" (for Propostional Attitude). An example of a belief attribution is given in (14).

(14) Mr. Marcus believes *spot steel prices will continue to fall through early 1990* **and** then **reverse themselves**. (0336)

	REL	Arg1	Arg2
[Source]	Ot	Inh	Inh
[Type]	PAtt	Null	Null

Facts are identified by the class of "factive and semi-factive verbs" (Kiparsky and Kiparsky, 1971; Karttunen, 1971) such as *regret*, *forget*, *remember*, *know*, *see*, *hear* etc. They take the value "Ftv" (for Factive) for *type* (Example 15). In the current scheme, this class does not distinguish between the true factives and semi-factives, the former involving an attitute/evaluation towards a fact, and the latter involving knowledge of a fact.

(15) The other side, he argues knows *Giuliani has always been pro-choice*, even though **he has personal reservations**. (0041)

	REL	Arg1	Arg2
[Source]	Ot	Inh	Inh
[Type]	Ftv	Null	Null

Lastly, *eventualities* are identified by a class of verbs which denote three kinds of relations between agents and eventualities (Sag and Pollard, 1991). The first kind is anchored by *verbs of influence* like *persuade*, *permit*, *order*, and involve one agent influencing another agent to perform (or not perform) an action. The second kind is anchored by *verbs of commitment* like *promise*, *agree*, *try*, *intend*, *refuse*, *decline*, and involve an agent committing to perform (or not perform) an action. Finally, the third kind is anchored by *verbs of orientation* like *want*, *expect*, *wish*, *yearn*, and involve desire, expectation, or some similar mental orientation towards some state(s) of affairs. These sub-distinctions are not encoded in the annotation, but we have used the definitions as a guide for identifying these predicates. All these three types are collectively referred to and annotated as *verbs of control*. *Type* for these classes takes the value "Ctrl" (for Control). Note that the syntactic term *control* is used because these verbs denote uniform structural control properties, but the primary basis for their definition is nevertheless semantic. An example of the control attribution relation anchored by a verb of influence is given in (16).

(16) Eward and Whittington had planned to leave the bank earlier, but Mr. Craven had persuaded them *to remain* until **the bank was in a healthy position**. (1949)

	REL	Arg1	Arg2
[Source]	Ot	Inh	Inh
[Type]	Ctrl	Null	Null

Note that while our use of the term *source* applies literally to agents responsible for the truth of a proposition, we continue to use the same term for the agents for facts and eventualities. Thus, for facts, the *source* represents the bearers of attitudes/knowledge, and for considered eventualities, the *source* represents intentions/attitudes.

3.3 Scopal Polarity

The *scopal polarity* feature is annotated on relations and their arguments to primarily identify cases when verbs of attribution are negated on the surface - syntactically (e.g., *didn't say*, *don't think*) or lexically (e.g., *denied*), but when the negation in fact reverses the polarity of the attributed relation or argument content (Horn, 1978). Example (17) illustrates such a case. The 'but' clause entails an interpretation such as "I think it's not a main consideration", for which the negation must take narrow scope over the embedded clause rather than the higher clause. In particular, the interpretation of the CONTRAST relation denoted by *but* requires that Arg2 should be interpreted under the scope of negation.

(17) *"Having the dividend increases is a supportive element in the market outlook,* but I don't think **it's a main consideration**," he says. (0090)

	REL	Arg1	Arg2
[Source]	Ot	Inh	Inh
[Type]	Comm	Null	PAtt
[Polarity]	Null	Null	Neg

To capture such entailments with surface negations on attribution verbs, an argument of a connective is marked "Neg" for *scopal polarity* when the interpretation of the connective requires the surface negation to take semantic scope over the lower argument. Thus, in Example (17), *scopal polarity* is marked as "Neg" for Arg2.

When the neg-lowered interpretations are not present, *scopal polarity* is marked as the default "Null" (such as for the relation and Arg1 of Example 17).

It is also possible for the surface negation of attribution to be interpreted as taking scope over the relation, rather than an argument. We have not observed this in the corpus yet, so we describe this case with the constructed example in (18). What the example shows is that in addition to entailing (18b) - in which case it would be annotated parallel to Example (17) above - (18a) can also entail (18c), such that the negation is intrepreted as taking semantic scope over the "relation" (Lasnik, 1975), rather than one of the arguments. As the *scopal polarity* annotations for (18c) show, lowering of the surface negation to the relation is marked as "Neg" for the *scopal polarity* of the relation.

(18) a. John doesn't think *Mary will get cured* because **she took the medication**.

b. $\models$ John thinks *that* because **Mary took the medication**, *she will not get cured.*

	REL	Arg1	Arg2
[Source]	Ot	Inh	Inh
[Type]	PAtt	Null	Null
[Polarity]	Null	Neg	Null

c. $\models$ John thinks *that Mary will get cured* not because **she took the medication** (but because she has started practising yoga.)

	REL	Arg1	Arg2
[Source]	Ot	Inh	Inh
[Type]	PAtt	Null	Null
[Polarity]	Neg	Null	Null

We note that *scopal polarity* does not capture the appearance of (opaque) internal negation that may appear on arguments or relations themselves. For example, a modified connective such as *not because* does not take "Neg" as the value for *scopal polarity*, but rather "Null". This is consistent with our goal of marking *scopal polarity* only for lowered negation, i.e., when surface negation from the attribution is lowered to either the relation or argument for interpretation.

3.4 Determinacy

The *determinacy* feature captures the fact that the entailment of the attribution relation can be made indeterminate in context, for example when it appears syntactically embedded in negated or conditional contexts.. The annotation attempts to capture such indeterminacy with the value "Indet". Determinate contexts are simply marked as the default "Null". For example, the annotation in (19) conveys the idea that the belief or opinion about the effect of higher salaries on teachers' performance is not really attributed to anyone, but is rather only being conjectured as a possibility.

(19) It is silly libel on our teachers to think *they would educate our children better* if only **they got a few thousand dollars a year more**. (1286)

	REL	Arg1	Arg2
[Source]	Ot	Inh	Inh
[Type]	PAtt	Null	Null
[Polarity]	Null	Null	Null
[Determinacy]	Indet	Null	Null

3.5 Attribution Spans

In addition to annotating the properties of attribution in terms of the features discussed above, we also propose to annotate the *text span* associated with the attribution. The text span is annotated as a single (possibly discontinuous) complex reflecting three of the annotated features, namely *source*, *type* and *scopal polarity*. The attribution span also includes all non-clausal modifiers of the elements contained in the span, for example, adverbs and appositive NPs. Connectives, however, are excluded from the span, even though they function as modifiers. Example (20) shows a discontinuous annotation of the attribution, where the parenthetical *he argues* is excluded from the attribution phrase *the other side knows*, corresponding to the factive attribution.

(20) The other side, he argues knows *Giuliani has always been pro-choice,* even though **he has personal reservations**. (0041)

	REL	Arg1	Arg2
[Source]	Ot	Inh	Inh
[Type]	Ftv	Null	Null
[Polarity]	Null	Null	Null
[Determinacy]	Null	Null	Null

Inclusion of the fourth feature, *determinacy*, is not "required" to be included in the current scheme because the entailment cancelling contexts can be very complex. For example, in Example (19), the conditional interpretation leading to the indeterminacy of the relation and its arguments is due to the syntactic construction type of the entire sentence. It is not clear how to annotate the indeterminacy induced by such contexts. In the example, therefore, the attribution span only includes the anchor for the *type* of the attribution.

Spans for implicit writer attributions are left unmarked since there is no corresponding text that can be selected. The absence of a span annotation is simply taken to reflect writer attribution, together with the "Wr" value on the source feature.

Recognizing attributions is not trivial since they are often left unexpressed in the sentence in which the AO is realized, and have to be inferred from the prior discourse. For example, in (21), the relation together with its arguments in the third sentence are attributed to Larry Shapiro, but this attribution is implicit and must be inferred from the first sentence.

(21) "There are certain cult wines that can command these higher prices," [says Larry Shapiro of Marty's, ...] "What's different is that it is happening with young wines just coming out. *We're seeing it* partly because **older vintages are growing more scarce**." (0071)

	REL	Arg1	Arg2
[Source]	Ot	Inh	Inh

The spans for such implicit "Ot" attributions mark the text that provides the inference of the implicit attribution, which is just the closest occurrence of the explicit attribution phrase in the prior text.

The final aspect of the span annotation is that we also annotate non-clausal phrases as the anchors attribution, such as prepositional phrases like *according to X*, and adverbs like *reportedly, allegedly, supposedly*. One such example is shown in (22).

(22) *No foreign companies bid on the Hiroshima project,* [*according to the bureau*]. But **the Japanese practice of deep discounting often is cited by Americans as a classic barrier to entry in Japan's market**. (0501)

	REL	Arg1	Arg2
[Source]	Wr	Ot	Inh
[Type]	Comm	Comm	Null
[Polarity]	Null	Null	Null
[Determinacy]	Null	Null	Null

Note that adverbials are free to pick their own *type* of attribution. For example, *supposedly* as an attribution adverb picks "PAtt" as the value for *type*.

3.6 Attribution of Implicit Relations

Implicit connectives and their arguments in the PDTB are also marked for attribution. Implicit connectives express relations that are inferred by the reader. In such cases, the writer intends for the reader to infer a discourse relation. As with Explicit connectives, implicit relations intended by the writer of the article are distinguished from those intended by some other agent introduced by the writer. For example, while the implicit relation in Example (23) is attributed to the writer, in Example (24), both `Arg1` and `Arg2` have been expressed by someone else whose speech is being quoted: in this case, the implicit relation is attributed to the other agent.

(23) *The gruff financier recently started socializing in upper-class circles.* `Implicit` = FOR EXAMPLE (ADD.INFO) Although he says he wasn't keen on going, **last year he attended a New York gala where his daughter made her debut**. (0800)

	REL	Arg1	Arg2
[Source]	Wr	Inh	Inh
[Type]	Comm	Null	Null
[Polarity]	Null	Null	Null
[Determinacy]	Null	Null	Null

(24) "*We asked police to investigate why they are allowed to distribute the flag in this way.* Implicit=BECAUSE (CAUSE) **It should be considered against the law**," [said Danny Leish, a spokesman for the association].

	REL	Arg1	Arg2
[Source]	Ot	Inh	Inh
[Type]	Comm	Null	Null
[Polarity]	Null	Null	Null
[Determinacy]	Null	Null	Null

For implicit relations, attribution is also annotated for AltLex relations but not for EntRel and NoRel, since the former but not the latter refer to the presense of discourse relations.

4 Summary

In this paper, we have proposed and described an annotation scheme for marking the attribution of both explicit and implicit discourse connectives and their arguments in the Penn Discourse TreeBank. We discussed the role of the annotations for the recognition of factuality in natural language applications, and defined the notion of attribution. The scheme was presented in detail with examples, outlining the "feature-based annotation" in terms of the *source*, *type*, *scopal polarity*, and *determinacy* associated with attribution, and the "span annotation" to highlight the text reflecting the attribution features.

Acknowledgements

The Penn Discourse TreeBank project is partially supported by NSF Grant: Research Resources, EIA 02-24417 to the University of Pennsylvania (PI: A. Joshi). We are grateful to Lukasz Abramowicz and the anonymous reviewers for useful comments.

References

Nicholas. Asher. 1993. *Reference to Abstract Objects in Discourse*. Kluwer, Dordrecht.

Nikhil Dinesh, Alan Lee, Eleni Miltsakaki, Rashmi Prasad, Aravind Joshi, and Bonnie Webber. 2005. Attribution and the (non)-alignment of syntactic and discourse arguments of connectives. In *Proceedings of the ACL Workshop on Frontiers in Corpus Annotation II: Pie in the Sky*, Ann Arbor, Michigan.

Jaakko Hintikka. 1971. Semantics for propositional attitudes. In L. Linsky, editor, *Reference and Modality*, pages 145–167. Oxford.

Laurence Horn. 1978. Remarks on neg-raising. In Peter Cole, editor, *Syntax and Semantics 9: Pragmatics*. Academic Press, New York.

Lauri Karttunen. 1971. Some observations on factivity. *Papers in Linguistics*, 4:55–69.

Carol Kiparsky and Paul Kiparsky. 1971. Fact. In D. D. Steinberg and L. A. Jakobovits, editors, *Semantics: An Interdisciplinary Reader in Philosophy, Linguistics and Psychology*, pages 345–369. Cambridge University Press, Cambridge.

Howard Lasnik. 1975. On the semantics of negation. In *Contemporary Research in Philosophical Logic and Linguistic Semantics*, pages 279–313. Dordrecht: D. Reidel.

Beth Levin. 1993. *English Verb Classes And Alternations: A Preliminary Investigation*. University of Chicago Press.

Mitchell P. Marcus, Beatrice Santorini, and Mary Ann Marcinkiewicz. 1993. Building a large annotated corpus of english: The Penn Treebank. *Computational Linguistics*, 19(2):313–330.

Eleni Miltsakaki, Rashmi Prasad, Aravind Joshi, and Bonnie Webber. 2004. Annotating discourse connectives and their arguments. In *Proceedings of the HLT/NAACL Workshop on Frontiers in Corpus Annotation*, pages 9–16, Boston, MA.

Bo Pang, Lillian Lee, and Shivakumar Vaithyanathan. 2002. Thumbs up? sentiment classification using machine learning techniques. In *Proceedings of the Conference on Empirical Methods in Natural Language Processing (EMNLP-2002)*, pages 79–86.

Rashmi Prasad, Eleni Miltsakaki, Aravind Joshi, and Bonnie Webber. 2004. Annotation and data mining of the Penn Discourse Treebank. In *Proceedings of the ACL Workshop on Discourse Annotation*, pages 88–95, Barcelona, Spain.

Rashmi Prasad, Aravind Joshi, Nikhil Dinesh, Alan Lee, Eleni Miltsakaki, and Bonnie Webber. 2005. The Penn Discourse TreeBank as a resource for natural language generation. In *Proceedings of the Corpus Linguistics Workshop on Using Corpora for NLG*.

Ellen Riloff, Janyce Wiebe, and Willian Phillips. 2005. Exploiting subjectivity classification to improve information extraction. In *Proceedings of the 20th National Conference on Artificial Intelligence (AAAI-2005)*.

Ivan A. Sag and Carl Pollard. 1991. An integrated theory of complement control. *Language*, 67(1):63–113.

The PDTB-Group. 2006. The Penn Discourse TreeBank 1.0 Annotation Manual. Technical Report IRCS-06-01, Institute for Research in Cognitive Science, University of Pennsylvania.

Veseli Stoyanov, Claire Cardie, and Janyce Wiebe. 2005. Multi-perspective question answering using the OpQA corpus. In *Proceedings of HLT-EMNLP*.

Peter D. Turney. 2002. Thumbs up or thumbs down? semantic orientation applied to unsupervised classification of reviews. In *Proceedings of ACL 2002*, pages 417–424.

Bonnie Webber, Aravind Joshi, M. Stone, and Alistair Knott. 2003. Anaphora and discourse structure. *Computational Linguistics*, 29(4):545–587.

Bonnie Webber, Aravind Joshi, Eleni Miltsakaki, Rashmi Prasad, Nikhil Dinesh, Alan Lee, and K. Forbes. 2005. A short introduction to the PDTB. In *Copenhagen Working Papers in Language and Speech Processing*.

Janyce Wiebe, Theresa Wilson, Rebecca Bruce, Matthew Bell, and Melanie Martin. 2004. Learning subjective language. *Computational Linguistics*, 30(3):277–308.

Janyce Wiebe, Theresa Wilson, , and Claire Cardie. 2005. Annotating expressions of opinions and emotions in language. *Language Resources and Evaluation*, 1(2).

Theresa Wilson and Janyce Wiebe. 2005. Annotating attributions and private states. In *Proceedings of the ACL Workshop on Frontiers in Corpus Annotation II: Pie in the Sky*, Ann Arbor, Michigan.

Hon Yu and Vasileios Hatzivassiloglou. 2003. Towards answering opinion questions: separating facts from opinions and identifying the polarity of opinion sentences. In *Proceedings of EMNLP-2003*, pages 129–136, Saporo, Japan.

Searching for Sentences Expressing Opinions by using Declaratively Subjective Clues

Nobuaki Hiroshima, Setsuo Yamada, Osamu Furuse and Ryoji Kataoka
NTT Cyber Solutions Laboratories, NTT Corporation
1-1 Hikari-no-oka Yokosuka-Shi Kanagawa, 239-0847 Japan
hiroshima.nobuaki@lab.ntt.co.jp

Abstract

This paper presents a method for searching the web for sentences expressing opinions. To retrieve an appropriate number of opinions that users may want to read, declaratively subjective clues are used to judge whether a sentence expresses an opinion. We collected declaratively subjective clues in opinion-expressing sentences from Japanese web pages retrieved with opinion search queries. These clues were expanded with the semantic categories of the words in the sentences and were used as feature parameters in a Support Vector Machine to classify the sentences. Our experimental results using retrieved web pages on various topics showed that the opinion expressing sentences identified by the proposed method are congruent with sentences judged by humans to express opinions.

1 Introduction

Readers have an increasing number of opportunities to read opinions (personal ideas or beliefs), feelings (mental states), and sentiments (positive or negative judgments) that have been written or posted on web pages such as review sites, personal web sites, blogs, and BBSes. Such subjective information on the web can often be a useful basis for finding out what people think about a particular topic or making a decision.

A number of studies on automatically extracting and analyzing product reviews or reputations on the web have been conducted (Dave et al., 2003; Morinaga et al., 2002; Nasukawa and Yi, 2003; Tateishi et al., 2004; Kobayashi et al., 2004). These studies focus on using sentiment analysis to extract positive or negative information about a particular product. Different kinds of subjective information, such as neutral opinions, requests, and judgments, which are not explicitly associated with positive/negative assessments, have not often been considered in previous work. Although sentiments provide useful information, opinion-expressing sentences like "In my opinion this product should be priced around $15," which do not express explicitly positive or negative judgments (unlike sentiments) can also be informative for a user who wants to know others' opinions about a product. When a user wants to collect opinions about an event, project, or social phenomenon, requests and judgments can be useful as well as sentiments. With open-domain topics, sentences expressing sentiments should not be searched exclusively; other kinds of opinion expressing sentences should be searched as well.

The goal of our research is to achieve a web search engine that locates opinion-expressing sentences about open-domain topics on products, persons, events, projects, and social phenomena. Sentence-level subjectivity/objectivity classification in some of the previous research (Riloff and Wiebe, 2003; Wiebe and Riloff, 2005) can identify subjective statements that include speculation in addition to positive/negative evaluations. In these efforts, the subjectivity/objectivity of a current sentence is judged based on the existence of subjective/objective clues in both the sentence itself and the neighboring sentences. The subjective clues, some adjective, some noun, and some verb phrases, as well as other collocations, are learned from corpora (Wiebe, 2000; Wiebe et al., 2001). Some of the clues express subjective meaning unrestricted to positive/negative measurements. The sentence-level subjectivity ap-

Proceedings of the Workshop on Sentiment and Subjectivity in Text, pages 39–46,
Sydney, July 2006. ©2006 Association for Computational Linguistics

proach suggests a way of searching for opinion expressing sentences in the open domain.

The problem of applying sentence-level subjectivity classification to opinion-expressing sentence searches is the likelihood of collecting too many sentences for a user to read. According to the work of Wiebe et al. (2001), 70% of sentences in opinion-expressing articles like editorials and 44% of sentences in non-opinion expressing articles like news reports were judged to be subjective. In analyzing opinions (Cardie et al., 2003; Wilson et al., 2004), judging document-level subjectivity (Pang et al., 2002; Turney, 2002), and answering opinion questions (Cardie et al., 2003; Yu and Hatzivassiloglou, 2003), the output of a sentence-level subjectivity classification can be used without modification. However, in searching opinion-expressing sentences, it is necessary to designate criteria for opinion-expressing sentences that limit the number of retrieved sentences so that a user can survey them without difficulty. While it is difficult to formally define an opinion, it is possible to practically tailor the definition of an opinion to the purpose of the application (Kim and Hovy, 2004).

This study introduces the notion of declaratively subjective clues as a criterion for judging whether a sentence expresses an opinion and proposes a method for finding opinion-expressing sentences that uses these clues. Declaratively subjective clues such as the subjective predicate part of the main clause and subjective sentential adverb phrases suggest that the writer is the source of the opinion. We hypothesize that a user of such an "opinion-expressing sentence" search wants to read the writer's opinions and that explicitly stated opinions are preferred over quoted or implicational opinions. We suppose that writer's ideas or beliefs are explicitly declared in a sentence with declaratively subjective clues whereas sentences without declaratively subjective clues mainly describe things. The number of sentences with declaratively subjective clues is estimated to be less than the number of subjective sentences defined in the previous work. We expect that the opinion expressing sentences identified with our method will be appropriate from the both qualitative and quantitative viewpoints.

Section 2 describes declaratively subjective clues and explains how we collected them from opinion-expressing sentences on Japanese web pages retrieved with opinion search queries. Section 3 explains our strategy for searching opinion-expressing sentences by using declaratively subjective clues. Section 4 evaluates the proposed method and shows how the opinion-expressing sentences found by the proposed method are congruent with the sentences judged by humans to be opinions.

2 Declaratively Subjective Clues

Declaratively subjective clues are a basic criterion for judging whether a sentence expresses an opinion. We extracted the declaratively subjective clues from Japanese sentences that evaluators judged to be opinions.

2.1 Opinion-expressing Sentence Judgment

We regard a sentence to be "opinion expressing" if it explicitly declares the writer's idea or belief at a sentence level. We define as a "declaratively subjective clue", the part of a sentence that contributes to explicitly conveying the writer's idea or belief in the opinion-expressing sentence. For example, "I am glad" in the sentence "I am glad to see you" can convey the writer's pleasure to a reader, so we regard the sentence as an "opinion-expressing sentence" and "I am glad" as a "declaratively subjective clue." Another example of a declaratively subjective clue is the exclamation mark in the sentence "We got a contract!" It conveys the writer's emotion about the event to a reader.

If a sentence only describes something abstract or concrete even though it has word-level or phrase-level subjective parts, we do not consider it to be opinion expressing. On the other hand, some word-level or phrase-level subjective parts can be declaratively subjective clues depending on where they occur in the sentence. Consider the following two sentences.

(1) This house is beautiful.
(2) We purchased a beautiful house.

Both (1) and (2) contain the word-level subjective part "beautiful". Our criterion would lead us to say that sentence (1) is an opinion, because "beautiful" is placed in the predicate part and (1) is considered to declare the writer's evaluation of the house to a reader. This is why "beautiful" in (1) is eligible as a declaratively subjective clue. On the other hand, sentence (2) is not judged to contain an opinion, because "beautiful" is placed in the noun phrase, i.e., the object of the verb "purchase," and (2) is considered to report the event of the house purchase rather objectively to a reader. Sentence (2) partially contains subjective information about the beauty of the house; however this information is unlikely to be what a writer wants to emphasize. Thus, "beautiful" in (2) does not work as a declaratively subjective clue.

These two sentences illustrate the fact that the presence of a subjective word ("beautiful") does not unconditionally assure that the sentence expresses an opinion. Additionally, these examples do suggest that sentences containing an opinion can be judged depending on where such word-level or phrase-level subjective parts as evaluative adjectives are placed in the predicate part.

Some word-level or phrase-level subjective parts such as subjective sentential adverbs can be declaratively subjective clues depending on where they occur in the sentence. In sentence (3), "amazingly" expresses the writer's feeling about the event. Sentence (3) is judged to contain an opinion because there is a subjective sentential adverb in its main clause.

(3) Amazingly, few people came to my party.

The existence of some idiomatic collocations in the main clause also affects our judgment as to what constitutes an opinion-expressing sentence. For example, sentence (4) can be judged as expressing an opinion because it includes "my wish is".

(4) My wish is to go abroad.

Thus, depending on the type of declaratively subjective clue, it is necessary to consider where the expression is placed in the sentence to judge whether the sentence is an opinion.

2.2 Clue Expression Collection

We collected declaratively subjective clues in opinion-expressing sentences from Japanese web pages. Figure 1 illustrates the flow of collection of eligible expressions.

type	query's topic
Product	cell phone, car, beer, cosmetic
Entertainment	sports, movie, game, animation
Facility	museum, zoo, hotel, shop
Politics	diplomacy, election
Phenomena	diction, social behavior
Event	firework, festival
Culture	artwork, book, music
Organization	company
Food	cuisine, noodle, ice cream
Creature	bird

Table 1: Topic Examples

First, we retrieved Japanese web pages from forty queries covering a wide range of topics such as products, entertainment, facilities, and phenomena, as shown in Table 1. We used queries on various topics because we wanted to acquire declaratively subjective clues for open-domain opinion web searches. Most of the queries contain proper nouns. These queries correspond to possible situations in which a user wants to retrieve opinions from web pages about a particular topic, such as "Cell phone X," "Y museum," and "Football coach Z's ability", where X, Y, and Z are proper nouns.

Next, opinion-expressing sentences were extracted from the top twenty retrieved web pages in each query, 800 pages in total. There were 75,575 sentences in these pages.

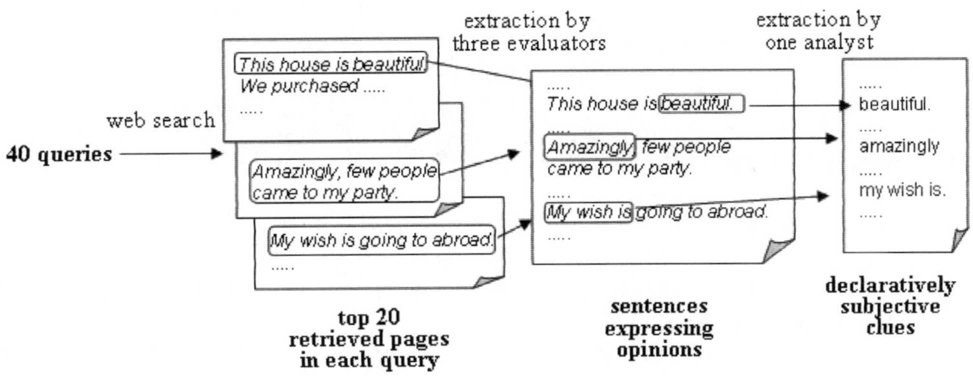

Figure 1: Flow of Clue Expression Collection

	type	example sentence (English translation of Japanese sentence)
(a)	Thought	*Kono hon wa kare no dato omou.* *(I think this book is his.)*
(b)	Declarative adverb	*Tabun rainen yooroppa ni iku.* *(I will possibly go to Europe next year.)*
(c)	Interjection	*Waa, suteki.* *(Oh, wonderful.)*
(d)	Intensifier	*Karera wa totemo jouzu ni asonda.* *(They played extremely well)*
(e)	Impression	*Kono yougo wa yayakoshii.* *(This terminology is confusing.)*
(f)	Emotion	*Oai dekite ureshii desu.* *(I am glad to see you.)*
(g)	Positive/negative judgment	*Anata no oodio kiki wa sugoi.* *(Your audio system is terrific.)*
(h)	Modality about propositional attitude	*Sono eiga wo miru beki da.* *(You should go to the movie.)*
(i)	Value judgment	*Kono bun wa imi fumei da.* *(This sentence makes no sense.)*
(j)	Utterance-specific sentence form	*Towa ittemo,ima wa tada no yume dakedo.* *(Though, it's literally just a dream now.)*
(k)	Symbol	*Keiyaku wo tottazo!* *(We got a contract!)*
(l)	Idiomatic collocation	*Ii nikui.* *(It's hard to say.)*
(m)	Uncertainty	*Ohiru ni nani wo tabeyou kanaa.* *(I am wondering what I should eat for lunch.)*
(n)	Imperative	*Saizen wo tukushi nasai.* *(Give it your best.)*

Table 2: Clue Types

Three evaluators judged whether each sentence contained an opinion or not. The 13,363 sentences judged to do so by all three evaluators were very likely to be opinion expressing. The number of sentences which three evaluators agreed on as non-opinion expressing was 42,346.[1] Out of the 13,363 opinion expressing sentences, 8,425 were then used to extract declaratively subjective clues and learn positive examples in a Support Vector Machine (SVM), and 4,938 were used to assess the performance of opinion expressing sentence search (Section 4). Out of the 42,346 non-opinion sentences, 26,340 were used to learn negative examples, and 16,006 were used to assess, keeping the number ratio of the positive and negative example sentences in learning and assessing.

One analyst extracted declaratively subjective clues from 8,425 of the 13,363 opinion-expressing sentences, and another analyst checked the result. The number of declaratively subjective clues obtained was 2,936. These clues were classified into fourteen types as shown in Table 2, where the underlined expressions in example sentences are extracted as declaratively subjective clues. The example sentences in Table 2 are Japanese opinion-expressing sentences and their English translations. Although some English counterparts of Japanese clue expressions might not be cogent because of the characteristic difference between Japanese and English, the clue types are likely to be language-independent. We can see that various types of expressions compose opinion-expressing sentences.

As mentioned in Section 2.1, it is important to check where a declaratively subjective clue appears in the sentence in order to apply our criterion of whether the sentence is an opinion or not. The clues in the types other than (b), (c) and (l) usually appear in the predicate part of a main clause.

The declaratively subjective clues in Japanese examples are placed in the rear parts of sentences except in types (b), (c) and (l). This reflects the heuristic rule that Japanese predicate

[1] Note that not all of these opinion-expressing sentences retrieved were closely related to the query because some of the pages described miscellaneous topics.

parts are in principle placed in the rear part of a sentence.

3 Opinion-Sentence Extraction

In this section, we explain the method of classifying each sentence by using declaratively subjective clues.

The simplest method for automatically judging whether a sentence is an opinion is a rule-based one that extracts sentences that include declaratively subjective clues. However, as mentioned in Section 2, the existence of declaratively subjective clues does not assure that the sentence expresses an opinion. It is a daunting task to write rules that describe how each declaratively subjective clue should appear in an opinion-expressing sentence. A more serious problem is that an insufficient collection of declaratively subjective clues will lead to poor extraction performance.

For that reason, we adopted a learning method that binarily classifies sentences by using declaratively subjective clues and their positions in sentences as feature parameters of an SVM. With this method, a consistent framework of classification can be maintained even if we add new declaratively subjective clues, and it is possible that we can extract the opinion-expressing sentences which have unknown declaratively subjective clues.

3.1 Augmentation by Semantic Categories

Before we can use declaratively subjective clues as feature parameters, we must address two issues:

- **Cost of building a corpus**: It is costly to provide a sufficient amount of tagged corpus of opinion-expressing-sentence labels to ensure that learning achieves a high-performance extraction capability.
- **Coverage of words co-occurring with declaratively subjective clues**: Many of the declaratively subjective clue expressions have co-occurring words in the opinion-expressing sentence. Consider the following two sentences.

  (5) The sky is high.
  (6) The quality of this product is high.

  Both (5) and (6) contain the word "high" in the predicate part. Sentence (5) is considered to be less of an opinion than (6) because an evaluator might judge (5) to be the objective truth, while all evaluators are likely to judge (6) to be an opinion. The adjective "high" in the predicate part can be validated as a declaratively subjective clue depending on co-occurring words. However, it is not realistic to provide all possible co-occurring words with each declaratively subjective clue expression.

Semantic categories can be of help in dealing with the above two issues. Declaratively subjective clue expressions can be augmented by semantic categories of the words in the expressions. An augmentation involving both declaratively subjective clues and co-occurrences will increase feature parameters. In our implementation, we adopted the semantic categories proposed by Ikehara et al. (1997). Utilization of semantic categories has another effect: it improves the extraction performance. Consider the following two sentence patterns:

(7) X is beautiful.
(8) X is pretty.

The words "beautiful" and "pretty" are adjectives in the common semantic category, "appearance", and the degree of declarative subjectivity of these sentences is almost the same regardless of what X is. Therefore, even if "beautiful" is learned as a declaratively subjective clue but "pretty" is not, the semantic category "appearance" that the learned word "beautiful" belongs to, enables (8) to be judged opinion expressing as well as (7).

3.2 Feature Parameters to Learn

We implemented our opinion-sentence extraction method by using a Support Vector Machine (SVM) because an SVM can efficiently learn the model for classifying sentences into opinion-expressing and non-opinion expressing, based on the combinations of multiple feature parameters. The following are the crucial feature parameters of our method.

- 2,936 declaratively subjective clues
- 2,715 semantic categories that words in a sentence can fall into

If the sentence has a declaratively subjective clue of type (b), (c) or (l) in Table 2, the feature parameter about the clue is assigned a value of 1; if not, it is assigned 0. If the sentence has declaratively subjective clues belonging to types

Method	Opinion			No opinion			Accuracy
	Precision	Recall	F-measure	Precision	Recall	F-measure	
Occurrences of DS clues (baseline 1)	66.4%	35.3%	46.0%	82.6%	94.5%	88.1%	80.5%
Bag of words (baseline 2)	**80.9%**	64.2%	71.6%	89.6%	**95.3%**	92.4%	88.0%
Proposed	78.6%	**70.8%**	**74.4%**	**91.3%**	94.0%	**92.6%**	**88.6%**

Table 4: Results for comparison with baseline methods

System \ Answer	Opinion	No opinion
Opinion	a	b
No opinion	c	d

Table 3: Number of sentences in a test set

other than (b), (c) or (l) in the predicate part, the feature parameter about the clue is assigned 1; if not, it is assigned 0.

The feature parameters for the semantic category are used to compensate for the insufficient amount of declaratively subjective clues provided and to consider co-occurring words with clue expressions in the opinion-expressing sentences, as mentioned in Section 3.1.

The following are additional feature parameters.

- 150 frequent words
- 13 parts of speech

Each feature parameter is assigned a value of 1 if the sentence has any of the frequent words or parts of speech. We added these feature parameters based on the hypotheses that some frequent words in Japanese have the function of changing the degree of declarative subjectivity, and that the existence of such parts of speech as adjectives and adverbs possibly influences the declarative subjectivity. The effectiveness of these additional feature parameters was confirmed in our preliminary experiment.

4 Experiments

We conducted three experiments to assess the validity of the proposed method: comparison with baseline methods, effectiveness of position information in SVM feature parameters, and effectiveness of SVM feature parameters such as declaratively subjective clues and semantic categories.

All experiments were performed using the Japanese sentences described in Section 2.1. We used 8,425 opinion expressing sentences, which were used to collect declaratively subjective clues as a training set, and used 4,938 opinion-expressing sentences as a test set. We also used 26,340 non-opinion sentences as a training set and used 16,006 non-opinion sentences as a test set. The test set was divided into ten equal subsets. The experiments were evaluated with the following measures following the variable scheme in Table 3:

$$P_{op} = \frac{a}{a+b} \qquad R_{op} = \frac{a}{a+c}$$

$$F_{op} = \frac{2P_{op}R_{op}}{P_{op}+R_{op}}$$

$$P_{no\_op} = \frac{d}{c+d} \qquad R_{no\_op} = \frac{d}{b+d}$$

$$F_{no\_op} = \frac{2P_{no\_op}R_{no\_op}}{P_{no\_op}+R_{no\_op}}$$

$$A = \frac{a+d}{a+b+c+d}$$

We evaluated ten subsets with the above measures and took the average of these results.

4.1 Comparison with Baseline Methods

We first performed an experiment comparing two baseline methods with our proposed method. We prepared a baseline method that regards a sentence as an opinion if it contains a number of declaratively subjective clues that exceeds a certain threshold. The best threshold was set through trial and error at five occurrences. We also prepared another baseline method that learns a model and classifies a sentence using only features about a bag of words.

The experimental results are shown in Table 4. It can be seen that our method performs better than the two baseline methods. Though the difference between our method's results and those of the bag-of-words method seems rather small, the superiority of the proposed method cannot be rejected at the significance level of 5% in t-test.

Position	Opinion			No opinion			Accuracy
	Precision	Recall	F-measure	Precision	Recall	F-measure	
All words	76.8%	70.6%	73.5%	91.2%	93.4%	92.3%	88.0%
Last 10 words	**78.6%**	**70.8%**	**74.4%**	**91.3%**	**94.0%**	**92.6%**	**88.6%**

Table 5: Results for feature parameters with position information

Feature sets		Opinion			No opinion			Accuracy
DS clues	Semantic categories	Precision	Recall	F-measure	Precision	Recall	F-measure	
		71.4%	53.2%	60.9%	87.7%	94.1%	90.8%	85.2%
Y		**79.9%**	64.3%	71.2%	89.6%	**95.0%**	92.2%	87.8%
	Y	76.1%	68.9%	72.2%	90.7%	93.3%	92.0%	87.5%
Y	Y	78.6%	**70.8%**	**74.4%**	**91.3%**	94.0%	**92.6%**	**88.6%**

Table 6: Results for effect of feature parameters

4.2 Feature Parameters with Position Information

We inspected the effect of position information of 2,936 declaratively subjective clues based on the heuristic rule that a Japanese predicate part almost always appears in the last ten words in a sentence. Instead of more precisely identifying predicate position from parsing information, we employed this heuristic rule as a feature parameter in the SVM learner for practical reasons.

Table 5 lists the experimental results. "All words" indicates that all feature parameters are permitted at any position in the sentence. "Last 10 words" indicates that all feature parameters are permitted only if they occur within the last ten words in the sentence.

We can see that feature parameters with position information perform better than those without position information in all evaluations. This result confirms our claim that the position of the feature parameters is important for judging whether a sentence is an opinion or not.

However, the difference did not indicate superiority between the two results at the significance level of 5%. In the “last 10 word” experiment, we restricted the position of 422 declaratively subjective clues like (b), (c) and (l) in Table 2, which appear in any position of a sentence, to the same conditions as with the other types of 2,514 declaratively subjective clues. The fact that the equal position restriction on all declaratively subjective clues slightly improved performance suggests there will be significant improvement in performance from assigning the individual position condition to each declaratively subjective clue.

4.3 Effect of Feature Parameters

The third experiment was designed to ascertain the effects of declaratively subjective clues and semantic categories. The declaratively subjective clues and semantic categories were employed as feature parameters for the SVM learner. The effect of each particular feature parameter can be seen by using it without the other feature parameter, because the feature parameters are independent of each other.

The experimental results are shown in Table 6. The first row shows trials using only frequent words and parts of speech as feature parameters. "Y" in the first and second columns indicates exclusive use of declaratively subjective clues and semantic categories as the feature parameters, respectively. For instance, we can determine the effect of declaratively subjective clues by comparing the first row with the second row.

The results show the effects of declaratively subjective clues and semantic categories. The results of the first row show that the method using only frequent words and parts of speech as the feature parameters cannot precisely classify subjective sentences. Additionally, the last row of the results clearly shows that using both declaratively subjective clues and semantic categories as the feature parameters is the most effective. The difference between the last row of the results and the other rows cannot be rejected even at the significance level of 5%.

5 Conclusion and Future Work

We proposed a method of extracting sentences classified by an SVM as opinion-expressing that uses feature sets of declaratively subjective clues collected from opinion-expressing sentences in Japanese web pages and semantic categories of words obtained from a Japanese lexicon. The first experiment showed that our method performed better than baseline methods. The second experiment suggested that our method performed better when extraction of features was limited to the predicate part of a sentence rather than allowed anywhere in the sentence. The last experiment showed that using both declaratively subjective clues and semantic categories as feature parameters yielded better results than using either clues or categories exclusively.

Our future work will attempt to develop an open-domain opinion web search engine. To succeed, we first need to augment the proposed opinion-sentence extraction method by incorporating the query relevancy mechanism. Accordingly, a user will be able to retrieve opinion-expressing sentences relevant to the query. Second, we need to classify extracted sentences in terms of emotion, sentiment, requirement, and suggestion so that a user can retrieve relevant opinions on demand. Finally, we need to summarize the extracted sentences so that the user can quickly learn what the writer wanted to say.

References

Claire Cardie, Janyce Wiebe, Theresa Wilson, and Diane J. Litman. 2003. *Combining Low-Level and Summary Representations of Opinions. for Multi-Perspective Question Answering.* Working Notes - New Directions in Question Answering (AAAI Spring Symposium Series) .

Kushal Dave, Steve Lawrence, and David M. Pennock. 2003. *Mining the peanut gallery: Opinion extraction and semantic classification of product reviews.* Proceedings of the 12th International World Wide Web Conference, 519-528.

Satoru Ikehara, Masahiro Miyazaki, Akio Yokoo, Satoshi Shirai, Hiromi Nakaiwa, Kentaro Ogura, Yoshifumi Ooyama, and Yoshihiko Hayashi. 1997. *Nihongo Goi Taikei – A Japanese Lexicon.* Iwanami Shoten. 5 volumes. (In Japanese).

Soo-Min Kim and Eduard Hovy. 2004. *Determining the Sentiment of Opinions.* Proceedings of the. COLING-04.

Nozomi Kobayashi, Kentaro Inui, Yuji Matsumoto, Kenji Tateishi, and Toshikazu Fukushima. 2004. *Collecting Evaluative Expressions for Opinion Extraction.* Proceedings of the First International Joint Conference on Natural Language Processing (IJCNLP-04), 584-589.

Satoshi Morinaga, Kenji Yamanishi, and Kenji Tateishi. 2002. *Mining Product Reputations on the Web.* Proceedings of the eighth ACM SIGKDD International Conference on Knowledge Discovery and Data Mining (KDD 2002).

Bo Pang, Lillian Lee, and Shivakumar Vaithyanathan. 2002. *Thumbs up? Sentiment Classification using Machine Learning Techniques.* Proceedings of the Conference on Empirical Methods in Natural Language Processing (EMNLP-2002), 76-86.

Tetsuya Nasukawa and Jeonghee Yi. 2003. *Sentiment Analysis: Capturing Favorability Using Natural Language Processing.* Proceedings of the 2nd International Conference on Knowledge Capture(K-CAP 2003).

Ellen Riloff and Janyce Wiebe. 2003. *Learning Extraction Patterns for Subjective Expressions.* Proceedings of the Conference on Empirical Methods in Natural Language Processing (EMNLP-03), 105-112.

Kenji Tateishi, Yoshihide Ishiguro, and Toshikazu Fukushima, 2004. *A Reputation Search Engine that Collects People's Opinions by Information Extraction Technology,* IPSJ Transactions Vol. 45 No.SIG07, 115-123.

Peter Turney. 2002. *Thumbs Up or Thumbs Down? Semantic Orientation Applied to Unsupervised Classification of Reviews.* Proceedings of the 40th Annual Meeting of the Association for Computational Linguistics (ACL-2002), 417-424.

Janyce Wiebe. 2000. *Learning Subjective Adjectives from Corpora.* Proceedings of the 17th National Conference on Artificial Intelligence (AAAI -2000).

Janyce Wiebe, Theresa Wilson, and Matthew Bell. 2001. *Identifying Collocations for Recognizing Opinions.* Proceedings of ACL/EACL 2001 Workshop on Collocation.

Janyce Wiebe and Ellen Riloff. 2005. *Creating Subjective and Objective Sentence Classifiers from Unannotated Texts.* Proceedings of Sixth International Conference on Intelligent Text Processing and Computational Linguistics (CICLing-2005), 486-497.

Theresa Wilson, Janyce Wiebe, and Rebecca Hwa, 2004. *Just how mad are you? Finding strong and weak opinion clauses.* Proceeding of the AAAI Spring Symposium on Exploring Attitude and Affect in Text: Theories and Applications.

Hong Yu and Vasileios Hatzivassiloglou. 2003. *Towards Answering Opinion Questions: Separating Facts from Opinions and Identifying the Polarity of Opinion Sentences.* Proceedings of the Conference on Empirical Methods in Natural Language Processing (EMNLP-2003).

Exploitation in Affect Detection in Open-Ended Improvisational Text

Li Zhang, John A. Barnden, Robert J. Hendley and Alan M. Wallington
School of Computer Science
University of Birmingham
Birmingham B15 2TT, UK
l.zhang@cs.bham.ac.uk

Abstract

We report progress on adding affect-detection to a program for virtual dramatic improvisation, monitored by a human director. We have developed an affect-detection module to control an automated virtual actor and to contribute to the automation of directorial functions. The work also involves basic research into how affect is conveyed through metaphor. The project contributes to the application of sentiment and subjectivity analysis to the creation of emotionally believable synthetic agents for interactive narrative environments.

1 Introduction

Improvised drama and role-play are widely used in education, counselling and conflict resolution. Researchers have explored frameworks for e-drama, in which virtual characters (avatars) interact under the control of human actors. The springboard for our research is an existing system (*edrama*) created by one of our industrial partners, Hi8us Midlands, used in schools for creative writing and teaching in various subjects. The experience suggests that e-drama helps students lose their usual inhibitions, because of anonymity etc. In *edrama*, characters are completely human-controlled, their speeches textual in speech bubbles, and their visual forms cartoon figures. The actors (users) are given a loose scenario within which to improvise, but are at liberty to be creative. There is also a human director, who constantly monitors the unfolding drama and can intervene by, for example, sending messages to actors, or by introducing and controlling a minor 'bit-part' character to interact with the main characters. But this places a heavy burden on directors, especially if they are, for example, teachers and unpracticed in the directorial role. One research aim is thus partially to automate the directorial functions, which importantly involve affect detection. For instance, a director may intervene when emotions expressed or discussed by characters are not as expected. Hence we have developed an affect-detection module. It has not yet actually been used for direction, but instead to control an automated bit-part actor, EMMA (emotion, metaphor and affect). The module identifies affect in characters' speeches, and makes appropriate responses to help stimulate the improvisation. Within affect we include: basic and complex *emotions* such as anger and embarrassment; *meta-emotions* such as desiring to overcome anxiety; *moods* such as hostility; and *value judgments* (of goodness, etc.). Although merely detecting affect is limited compared to extracting full meaning, this is often enough for stimulating improvisation.

Much research has been done on creating affective virtual characters in interactive systems. Indeed, Picard's work (2000) makes great contributions to building affective virtual characters. Also, emotion theories, particularly that of Ortony, et al. (1988) (OCC), have been used widely therein. Egges et al. (2003) have provided virtual characters with conversational emotional responsiveness. However, few systems are aimed at detecting affect as broadly as we do and in open-ended utterances. Although Façade (Mateas, 2002) included processing of open-ended utterances, the broad detection of emotions, rudeness and value judgements is not covered. Zhe & Boucouvalas (2002) demonstrated emotion extraction using a tagger and a chunker to help detect the speaker's own emotions. But it focuses only on emotional adjectives, considers only

Proceedings of the Workshop on Sentiment and Subjectivity in Text, pages 47–54,
Sydney, July 2006. ©2006 Association for Computational Linguistics

first-person emotions and neglects deep issues such as figurative expression. Our work is distinctive in several respects. Our interest is not just in (a) the positive first-person case: the affective states that a virtual character X implies that it has (or had or will have, etc.), but also in (b) affect that X implies it lacks, (c) affect that X implies that other characters have or lack, and (d) questions, commands, injunctions, etc. concerning affect. We aim also for the software to cope partially with the important case of metaphorical conveyance of affect (Fussell & Moss, 1998; Kövecses, 1998).

Our project does not involve using or developing deep, scientific models of how emotional states, etc., function in cognition. Instead, the deep questions investigated are on linguistic matters such as the metaphorical expression of affect. Also, in studying how people understand and talk about affect, what is of prime importance is their common-sense views of how affect works, irrespective of scientific reality. Metaphor is strongly involved in such views.

2 Our Current Affect Detection

Various characterizations of emotion are used in emotion theories. The OCC model uses emotion labels (anger, etc.) and intensity, while Watson and Tellegen (1985) use positivity and negativity of affect as the major dimensions. Currently, we use an evaluation dimension (negative-positive), affect labels, and intensity. Affect labels plus intensity are used when strong text clues signalling affect are detected, while the evaluation dimension plus intensity is used for weak text clues. Moreover, our analysis reported here is based on the transcripts of previous e-drama sessions. Since even a person's interpretations of affect can be very unreliable, our approach combines various weak relevant affect indicators into a stronger and more reliable source of information for affect detection. Now we summarize our affect detection based on multiple streams of information.

2.1 Pre-processing Modules

The language in the speeches created in e-drama sessions severely challenges existing language-analysis tools if accurate semantic information is sought even for the purposes of restricted affect-detection. The language includes misspellings, ungrammaticality, abbreviations (often as in text messaging), slang, use of upper case and special punctuation (such as repeated exclamation marks) for affective emphasis, repetition of letters or words also for affective emphasis, and open-ended interjective and onomatopoeic elements such as "hm" and "grrrr". In the examples we have studied, which so far involve teenage children improvising around topics such as school bullying, the genre is similar to Internet chat.

To deal with the misspellings, abbreviations, letter repetitions, interjections and onomatopoeia, several types of pre-processing occur before actual detection of affect.

A lookup table has been used to deal with abbreviations e.g. 'im (I am)', 'c u (see you)' and 'l8r (later)'. It includes abbreviations used in Internet chat rooms and others found in an analysis of previous edrama sessions. We handle ambiguity (e.g.,"2" (to, too, two) in "I'm 2 hungry 2 walk") by considering the POS tags of immediately surrounding words. Such simple processing inevitably leads to errors, but in evaluations using examples in a corpus of 21695 words derived from previous transcripts we have obtained 85.7% accuracy, which is currently adequate. We are also considering dealing with abbreviations, etc. in a more general way by including them as special lexical items in the lexicon of the robust parser we are using (see below).

The iconic use of word length (corresponding roughly to imagined sound length) as found both in ordinary words with repeated letters (e.g. 'seeeee') and in onomatopoeia and interjections, (e.g. 'wheee', 'grr', 'grrrrrr', 'agh', 'aaaggghhh') normally implies strong affective states. We have a small dictionary containing base forms of some special words (e.g. 'grr') and some ordinary words that often have letters repeated in e-drama. Then the Metaphone spelling-correction algorithm (http://aspell.net/metaphone/), which is based on pronunciation, works with the dictionary to locate the base forms of words with letter repetitions.

Finally, the Levenshtein distance algorithm (http://www.merriampark.com/ld.htm) with a contemporary English dictionary deals with spelling mistakes in users' input.

2.2 Processing of Imperative Moods

One useful pointer to affect is the use of imperative mood, especially when used without softeners such as 'please' or 'would you'. Strong emotions and/or rude attitudes are often expressed in this case. There are special, common imperative phrases we deal with explicitly, such as "shut up" and "mind your own business". They usually indicate strong negative emotions. But the phenomenon is more general.

Detecting imperatives accurately in general is by itself an example of the non-trivial problems we face. We have used the syntactic output from the Rasp parser (Briscoe & Carroll, 2002) and semantic information in the form of the semantic profiles for the 1,000 most frequently used English words (Heise, 1965) to deal with certain types of imperatives.

Rasp recognises some types of imperatives directly. Unfortunately, the grammar of the 2002 version of the Rasp parser that we have used does not deal properly with certain imperatives (John Carroll, p.c), which means that examples like "you shut up", "Dave bring me the menu", "Matt don't be so blunt" and "please leave me alone", are not recognized as imperatives, but as normal declarative sentences. Therefore, further analysis is needed to detect imperatives, by additional processing applied to the possibly-incorrect syntactic trees produced by Rasp.

If Rasp outputs a subject, 'you', followed by certain verbs (e.g. 'shut', 'calm', etc) or certain verb phrases (e.g. 'get lost', 'go away' etc), the sentence type will be changed to imperative. (Note: in "you get out" the "you" could be a vocative rather than the subject of "get", especially as punctuation such as commas is often omitted in our genre; however these cases are not worth distinguishing and we assume that the "you" is a subject.) If a softener 'please' is followed by the base forms of a verb, then the input is taken to be imperative. If a singular proper noun is followed by a base form of the verb, then this sentence is taken to be an imperative as well (e.g. "Dave get lost"). However, when a subject is followed by a verb for which there is no difference at all between the base form and the past tense form, then ambiguity arises between imperative and declarative (e.g. "Lisa hit me").

There is an important special case of this ambiguity. If the object of the verb is 'me', then in order to solve the ambiguity, we have adopted the evaluation value of the verb from Heise's (1965) compilation of semantic differential profiles. In these profiles, Heise listed values of evaluation, activation, potency, distance from neutrality, etc. for the 1,000 most frequently used English words. In the evaluation dimension, positive values imply goodness. Because normally people tend to use 'a negative verb + me' to complain about an unfair fact to the others, if the evaluation value is negative for such a verb, then this sentence is probably not imperative but declarative (e.g. "Mayid hurt me"). Otherwise, other factors implying imperative are checked in this sentence, such as exclamation marks and capitalizations. If these factors occur, then the input is probably an imperative. Otherwise, the conversation logs are checked to see if there is any question sentence directed toward this speaker recently. If there is, then the input is conjectured to be declarative.

There is another type of sentence: 'don't you + base form of verb' that we have started to address. Though such a sentence is often interrogative, it is also often a negative version of an imperative with a 'you' subject (e.g. "Don't you dare call me a dog," "Don't you call me a dog"). Normally Rasp regards it as a question sentence. Thus, further analysis has also been implemented for such a sentence structure to change its sentence type to imperative. Although currently this has limited effect, as we only infer a (negative) affective quality when the verb is "dare", we plan to add semantic processing in an attempt to glean affect more generally from "Don't you ..." imperatives.

2.3 Affect Detection by Pattern Matching

In an initial stage of our work, affect detection was based purely on textual pattern-matching rules that looked for simple grammatical patterns or templates partially involving lists of specific alternative words. This continues to be a core aspect of our system but we have now added robust parsing and some semantic analysis. Jess, a rule-based Java framework, is used to implement the pattern/template-matching rules in EMMA.

In the textual pattern-matching, particular keywords, phrases and fragmented sentences are found, but also certain partial sentence structures are extracted. This procedure possesses the robustness and flexibility to accept many ungrammatical fragmented sentences and to deal with the varied positions of sought-after phraseology in speeches. However, it lacks other types of generality and can be fooled when the phrases are suitably embedded as subcomponents of other grammatical structures. For example, if the input is "I doubt she's really angry", rules looking for anger in a simple way will fail to provide the expected results.

The transcripts analysed to inspire our initial knowledge base and pattern-matching rules were derived independently from previous *edrama* improvisations based on a school bullying scenario. We have also worked on another, distinctly different scenario, Crohn's disease, based on a TV programme by another of our industrial partners (Maverick TV). The rule sets created for one scenario have a useful degree of applicability to other scenarios, though there will be a few changes in the related knowledge database according to the nature of specific scenarios.

The rules, as we mentioned at the beginning of this section, conjecture the character's emotions, evaluation dimension (negative or positive), politeness (rude or polite) and what response EMMA should make.

Multiple exclamation marks and capitalisation are frequently employed to express emphasis in e-drama sessions. If exclamation marks or capitalisation are detected in a character's utterance, then the emotion intensity is deemed to be comparatively high (and emotion is suggested even in the absence of other indicators).

A reasonably good indicator that an inner state is being described is the use of 'I' (see also Craggs & Wood (2004)), especially in combination with the present or future tense. In the school-bullying scenario, when 'I' is followed by a future-tense verb the affective state 'threatening' is normally being expressed; and the utterance is usually the shortened version of an implied conditional, e.g., "I'll scream [if you stay here]." Note that when 'I' is followed by a present-tense verb, a variety of other emotional states tend to be expressed, e.g. "I want my mum" (fear) and "I hate you" (dislike), I like you (liking). Further analysis of first-person, present-tense cases is provided in the following section.

2.4 Going Beyond Pattern Matching

In order to go beyond the limitations of simple pattern matching, sentence type information obtained from the Rasp parser has also been adopted in the pattern-matching rules. The general sentence structure information not only helps EMMA to detect affective states in the user's input (see the above discussion of imperatives), and to decide if the detected affective states should be counted, but also helps EMMA to make appropriate responses. Rasp will inform the pattern-matching rule with sentence type information. If the current input is a conditional or question sentence with affective keywords or structures in, then the affective states won't be valued. For example, if the input is "I like the place when it is quiet", Rasp works out its sentence type: a conditional sentence and the rule for structures containing 'like' with a normal declarative sentence label won't be activated. Instead, the rule for the keyword 'when' with a conditional sentence type label will be fired. Thus an appropriate response will be obtained.

Additionally, as we discussed in section 2.2, we use Rasp to indicate imperative sentences, such as when Mayid (the bully) said "Lisa, don't tell Miss about it". The pseudo-code example rule for such input is as follows:

(defrule example_rule

?fact <- (any string containing negation and the sentence type is 'imperative') =>

(obtain affect and response from knowledge database)

Thus the declarative input such as "I won't tell Miss about it" won't be able to activate the example rule due to different sentence type information. Especially, we have assigned a special sentence type label ('imp+please') for imperatives with softener 'please'. Only using this special sentence type label itself in the pattern-matching rule helps us effortlessly to obtain the user's linguistic style ('polite') and probably a polite response from EMMA as well according to different roles in specific scenarios.

Aside from using the Rasp parser, we have also worked on implementing simple types of semantic extraction of affect using affect dictionaries and electronic thesauri, such as WordNet. The way we are currently using WordNet is briefly as follows.

2.5 Using WordNet for a First Person Case

As we mentioned earlier, use of the first-person with a present-tense verb tends to express an affective state in the speaker, especially in discourse in which affect is salient, as is the case in scenarios such as School Bullying and Crohn's Disease. We have used the Rasp parser to detect such a sentence. First of all, such user's input is sent to the pattern-matching rules in order to obtain the speaker's current affective state and EMMA's response to the user. If there is no rule fired (i.e. we don't obtain any information of the speaker's affective state and EMMA's response from the pattern-matching rules), further processing is applied. We use WordNet to track down the rough synonyms of the verb (possibly from different WordNet "synsets") in the verb phrase of the input sentence, in order to allow a higher degree of generality than would be achieved just with the use of our pattern-matching rules. In order to find the closest synonyms to the verb in different synsets, the semantic profiles of the 1,000 most frequently used English words (Heise, 1965) have been employed, especially to find the evaluation values of every synonym of the original verb. We transform positive and negative evaluation values in Heise's dictionary into binary 'positive' and 'negative' only. Thus if any synonym has the same evaluation value ('positive' or 'negative') as that of the original verb, then it will be selected as a member of the set of closest synonyms. Then, we use one closest synonym to replace the original verb in the user's input. This newly built sentence will be sent to the pattern-matching rules in order to obtain the user's affective state and EMMA's response. Such processing (using a closest synonym to replace the original verb and sending the newly built sentence to the pattern-matching rules) continues until we obtain the speaker's affective state and appropriate response.

2.6 Responding Regimes

EMMA normally responds to, on average, every Nth speech by another character in the e-drama session, where N is a changeable parameter (currently set to 3). However, it also responds when EMMA's character's name is mentioned, and makes no response if it cannot detect anything useful in the utterance it is responding to. The one-in-N average is achieved by sampling a random variable every time another character says something. As a future development, we plan to have N dynamically adjustable according to how confident EMMA is about what it has discerned in the utterance at hand.

EMMA sometimes makes a random response from several stored response candidates that are suitable for the affective quality it has discerned in an utterance it is responding to. In addition, EMMA sometimes reflects back, in modified form, part of the user's input string as a subcomponent of its response. Notice here that, because the pre-processing module reported in section 2.1 expands abbreviations and corrects misspellings, it helps to obscure the fact that part of EMMA's response is only a reflection. E.g.:

<Character> I'm ur (*your*) best m8 (*mate*).

<EMMA> Why are you my best mate?

On the other hand, we also, on a random basis, purposely put phenomena such as abbreviations and Internet-chat features in EMMA's responses in order to make EMMA express itself more like a typical school-student user. E.g.:

<Character> You get lost!

<EMMA> Hey, coool it folks. (notice the lengthening of 'cool')

<Character> He didn't do it.

<EMMA> No1 believes you, m8. (where 'no1' stands for 'no one')

It should be borne in mind that EMMA's responses are not aimed at engaging with the detailed meaning of the utterance, but simply to stimulate the improvisation in a way that is somewhat sensitive to affect being expressed. Furthermore, in order to make the EMMA character's responses push the improvisation forward, the character will not only ask scenario related questions to the main characters, but also introduce new topics closely related to the scenario in the improvisation. In a recent user-testing debrief session, secondary school students mentioned that the human bit-part character did not stay in character and said pointless things, while in another session one student, who played a main character, believed that the EMMA character was the only one that stuck to scenario related topics. The directors reported that, even when a main character was silent and the director did not intervene very much, the EMMA character led the improvisation on the right track by raising new topics other characters were concerned about.

3 Affect via Metaphor

In the introduction we commented on two functions of metaphor. Metaphor is often used to convey affect and it also partly underlies folk theories of how affect and emotion work. As an example of the latter, folk theories of anger often talk about, and appear to conceive of, anger as if it were a heated fluid possibly exerting a strong pressure on its containing body. This motivates a wide range of metaphorical expressions both conventional such as "he was boiling with anger and about to blow his top" and more creative variants such as "the temperature in the office was getting higher and this had nothing to do with where the thermostat was set" (modified, slightly from a Google™ search). Passion, or lack of, is also often described in terms of heat and the latter example could in certain contexts be used in this manner. So far, examples of actors reflecting or commenting on the nature of their or others emotions, which would require an appropriate vocabulary, have been infrequent in the e-drama transcripts, although we might expect to find more examples as more students participate in the Crohn's disease scenario.

However, such metaphorically motivated folk models often directly motivate the terminology used to convey affect, as in utterances such as "you leave me cold", which conveys lack of interest or disdain. This use of metaphor to motivate folk models of emotions and, as a consequence, certain forms of direct expression of emotion has been extensively studied, albeit usually from a theoretical, linguistic, perspective (Fussell & Moss, 1998; Kövecses, 1998).

Less recognised (although see Barnden et al., 2004; Wallington et al., 2006) is the fact that metaphor is also frequently used to convey emotion more indirectly. Here the metaphor does not describe some aspect of an emotional state, but something else. Crucially, however, it also conveys a negative or positive value judgement which is carried over to what is being described and this attitude hints at the emotion. For example to say of someone's room that "it is a cess-pit" allows the negative evaluation of 'cess-pit' to be transferred to 'the room' and we might assume an emotion of disgust. In our transcripts we find examples such as "smelly attitude" and "you buy your clothes at the rag market" (which we take to be not literally true). Animal insults such as "you pig" frequently take this form, although many are now highly conventionalised. Our analysis of e-drama transcripts shows that this type of metaphor that conveys affect indirectly is much more common than the direct use.

It should be apparent that even though conventional metaphorical phraseology may well be listed in specialised lexicons, approaches to metaphor and affect which rely upon a form of lexical look-up to determine the meaning of utterances are likely to miss both the creative variants and extensions of standard metaphors and also the quite general carrying over of affectual evaluations from the literal meaning of an utterance to the intended metaphorical meaning.

At the time of writing (early June 2006) little in the way of metaphor handling has been incorporated into the EMMA affect-detection module. However, certain aspects of metaphor handling will be incorporated shortly, since they involve extensions of existing capabilities. Our intended approach is partly to look for stock metaphorical phraseology and straightforward variants of it, which is the most common form of metaphor in most forms of discourse, including e-drama. However, we also plan to employ a simple version of the more open-ended, reasoning-based techniques described in the ATT-Meta project on metaphor processing (Barnden et al., 2004; Wallington et al., 2006).

As a first step, it should be noted that insults and swear words are often metaphorical. We are currently investigating specialised insult dictionaries and the machine-readable version of the OALD, which indicates slang.

Calling someone an animal of any sort usually conveys affect, but it can be either insulting or affectionate. We have noted that calling someone the young of an animal is often affectionate, and the same is true of diminutive (e.g., 'piglet') and nursery forms (e.g., 'moo cow'), even when the adult form of the animal is usually used as an insult. Thus calling someone 'a cat' or 'catty' is different from describing them as kittenish. Likewise, "you young pup" is different from "you dog". We are constructing a dictionary of specific animals used in slang and as insults, but, more generally, for animals not listed we can use WordNet and electronic dictionaries to determine whether or not it is the young or mature form of the animal that is being used.

We have already noted that in metaphor the affect associated with a source term will carry across to the target by default. EMMA already consults Heise's compilation of semantic differential profiles for the evaluation value of the verb. We will extend the determination of the evaluation value to all parts of speech.

Having the means to determine the emotion conveyed by a metaphor is most useful when metaphor can be reliably spotted. There are a number of means of doing this for some metaphors. For example, idioms are often metaphorical (Moon 1988). Thus we can use an existing idiom dictionary, adding to it as necessary. This will work with fixed idioms, but, as is often noted, idioms frequently show some degree of variation, either by using synonyms of standard lexis, e.g., '**constructing** castles in the air' instead of 'building castles in the air', or by adding modifiers, e.g., 'shut your **big fat** mouth'. This variability will pose a challenge if one is looking for fixed expressions from an idiom dictionary. However, if the idiom dictionary is treated as providing base forms, with for example the nouns being treated as the head nouns of a noun-phrase, then the Rasp parser can be used to determine the noun phrase and the modifiers of the head noun, and likewise with verbs, verb-phrases, etc. Indeed, this approach can be extended beyond highly fixed expressions to other cases of metaphor, since as Deignan (2005) has noted metaphors tend to display a much greater degree of fixedness compared to non-metaphors, whilst not being as fixed as what are conventionally called idioms.

There are other ways of detecting metaphors which we could utilise. Thus, metaphoricity signals (as in Goatly, 1997; Wallington et al., 2003) signal the use of a metaphor in some cases. Such signals include phrases such as: *so to speak, sort of, almost, picture as*. Furthermore, semantic restriction violations (Wilks, 1978; Fass, 1997; Mason, 2004), as in "my car **drinks** petrol," often indicate metaphor, although not all metaphors violate semantic restrictions. To determine whether semantic restrictions are being violated, domain information from ontologies/thesauri such as WordNet could be used and/or statistical techniques as used by Mason (2004).

4 User Testing

We conducted a two-day pilot user test with 39 secondary school students in May 2005, in order to try out and a refine a testing methodology. The aim of the testing was primarily to measure the extent to which having EMMA as opposed to a person play a character affects users' level of enjoyment, sense of engagement, etc. We concealed the fact that EMMA was involved in some sessions in order to have a fair test of the difference that is made. We obtained surprisingly good results. Having a minor bit-part character called "Dave" played by EMMA as opposed to a person made no statistically significant difference to measures of user engagement and enjoyment, or indeed to user perceptions of the worth of the contributions made by the character "Dave". Users did comment in debriefing sessions on some utterances of Dave's, so it was not that there was a lack of effect simply because users did not notice Dave at all. Also, the frequencies of human "Dave" and EMMA "Dave" being responded to during the improvisation (sentences of Dave's causing a response divided by all sentences said by "Dave") are both roughly around 30%, again suggesting that users notice Dave. Additionally, the frequencies of other side-characters being responded to are roughly the same as the "Dave" character – "Matthew": around 30% and "Elise": around 35%.

Furthermore, it surprised us that no user appeared to realize that sometimes Dave was computer-controlled. We stress, however, that it is not an aim of our work to ensure that human actors do not realize this. More extensive, user testing at several Birmingham secondary schools is being conducted at the time of writing this paper, now that we have tried out and somewhat modified the methodology.

The experimental methodology used in the testing is as follows, in outline. Subjects are 14-16 year old students at local Birmingham schools. Forty students are chosen by each school for the testing. Four two-hour sessions take place at the school, each session involving a different set of ten students. In a session, the main phases are as follows: an introduction to the software; a First Improvisation Phase, where five students are involved in a School Bullying improvisation and the remaining five in a Crohn's Disease improvisation; a Second Improvisation Phase in which this assignment is reversed; filling out of a questionnaire by the students; and finally a group discussion acting as a debrief phase. For each improvisation, characters are pre-assigned to specific students. Each Improvisation Phase involves some preliminaries followed by ten minutes of improvisation proper.

In half of the SB improvisations and half of the CD improvisations, the minor character Dave is played by one of the students, and by EMMA in the remaining. When EMMA plays Dave, the student who would otherwise have played him is instructed to sit at another student's terminal and thereby to be an audience member. Students are told that we are interested in the experiences of audience members as well as of actors. Almost without exception students have appeared not to have suspected that having an audience member results from not having Dave played by another student. At the end of one exceptional session some students asked whether one of the directors from Hi8us was playing Dave.

Of the two improvisations a given student is involved in, exactly one involves EMMA playing Dave. This will be the first session or the second. This EMMA-involvement order and the order in which the student encounters SB and CD are independently counterbalanced across students.

The questionnaire is largely composed of questions that are explicitly about students' feelings about the experience (notably enjoyment, nervousness, and opinions about the worth of the dramatic contributions of the various characters), with essentially the same set of questions being asked separately about the SB and the CD improvisations. The other data collected are: for each debrief phase, written minutes and an audio and video record; notes taken by two observers present during each Improvisation Phase; and automatically stored transcripts of the sessions themselves, allowing analysis of linguistic forms used and types of interactivity. To date only the non-narrative questionnaire answers have been subjected to statistical analysis, with the sole independent variable being the involvement or otherwise of EMMA in improvisations.

5 Conclusion and Ongoing Work

We have implemented a limited degree of affect-detection in an automated bit-part character in an e-drama application, and fielded the actor successfully in pilot user-testing. Although there is a considerable distance to go in terms of the practical affect-detection that we plan to implement, the already implemented detection is able to cause reasonably appropriate contributions by the automated character. We also intend to use the affect-detection in a module for automatically generating director messages to human actors.

In general, our work contributes to the issue of how affect/sentiment detection from language can contribute to the development of believable responsive AI characters, and thus to a user's feeling of involvement in game playing. Moreover, the development of affect detection and sentiment & subjectivity analysis provides a good test-bed for the accompanying deeper research into how affect is conveyed linguistically.

Acknowledgement

The project is supported by grant RES-328-25-0009 under the ESRC/EPSRC/DTI "PACCIT" programme, and its metaphor aspects also by EPSRC grant EP/C538943/1. We thank our partners—Hi8us, Maverick TV and BT—and colleagues W.H. Edmondson, S.R. Glasbey, M.G. Lee and Z. Wen.

References

Barnden, J.A., Glasbey, S.R., Lee, M.G. & Wallington, A.M. 2004. Varieties and Directions of Interdomain Influence in Metaphor. *Metaphor and Symbol, 19(1)*, pp.1-30.

Briscoe, E. & J. Carroll. 2002. Robust Accurate Statistical Annotation of General Text. In *Proceedings of the 3rd International Conference on Language Resources and Evaluation*, Las Palmas, Gran Canaria. pp.1499-1504.

Craggs, R. & Wood. M. 2004. A Two Dimensional Annotation Scheme for Emotion in Dialogue. In *Proceedings of AAAI Spring Symposium: Exploring Attitude and Affect in Text.*

Deignan , A. 2005. *Metaphor and corpus Linguistics.* John Benjamins.

Egges, A., Kshirsagar, S. & Magnenat-Thalmann, N. 2003. A Model for Personality and Emotion Simulation, In *Proceedings of Knowledge-Based Intelligent Information & Engineering Systems (KES2003)*, Lecture Notes in AI. Springer-Verlag.

Fussell, S. & Moss, M. 1998. Figurative Language in Descriptions of Emotional States. In S. R. Fussell and R. J. Kreuz (Eds.), *Social and cognitive approaches to interpersonal communication.* Lawrence Erlbaum.

Fass, D. 1997. *Processing metaphor and metonymy.* Greenwich, Connecticut: Ablex

Goatly, A. 1997. *The language of metaphors.* Routledge London and New York:

Heise, D. R. 1965. Semantic Differential Profiles for 1,000 Most Frequent English Words. *Psychological Monographs* 79, pp.1-31.

Kövecses, Z. 1998. Are There Any Emotion-Specific Metaphors? In *Speaking of Emotions: Conceptualization and Expression.* Athanasiadou, A. and Tabakowska, E. (eds.), Berlin and New York: Mouton de Gruyter, pp.127-151.

Mason, Z.J. 2004. CorMet: a computational, corpus-based conventional metaphor extraction system. *Computational Linguistics 30:1.* pp. 23-44.

Mateas, M. 2002. Ph.D. Thesis. *Interactive Drama, Art and Artificial Intelligence.* School of Computer Science, Carnegie Mellon University.

Moon, R. 1998. *Fixed idioms and expressions in English.* Clarendon Press: Oxford, U.K

Ortony, A., Clore, G.L. & Collins, A. 1988. *The Cognitive Structure of Emotions.* CUP

Picard, R.W. 2000. Affective Computing. The MIT Press. Cambridge MA.

Sharoff, S. 2005. How to Handle Lexical Semantics in SFL: a Corpus Study of Purposes for Using Size Adjectives. *Systemic Linguistics and Corpus.* London: Continuum.

Watson, D. & Tellegen, A. 1985. Toward a Consensual Structure of Mood. *Psychological Bulletin*, 98, pp.219-235.

Zhe, X. & Boucouvalas, A. C. 2002. Text-to-Emotion Engine for Real Time Internet Communication. In *Proceedings of International Symposium on Communication Systems, Networks and DSPs,* Staffordshire University, UK, pp.164-168.

Wallington, A.M., Barnden, J.A., Barnden, M.A., Ferguson, F.J. & Glasbey, S.R. 2003. Metaphoricity Signals: A Corpus-Based Investigation. Technical Report CSRP-03-5, School of Computer Science, The University of Birmingham, U.K.

Wallington, A.M., Barnden, J.A. Glasbey S.R. and Lee M. G. 2006. Metaphorical reasoning with an economical set of mappings. *Delta*, 22:1

Wilks, Y. (1978). Making preferences more active. *Artificial Intelligence*, 10, pp. 75- 97

Towards a validated model for affective classification of texts

Michel Généreux and Roger Evans
Natural Language Technology Group (NLTG)
University of Brighton, United Kingdom
{M.Genereux,R.P.Evans}@brighton.ac.uk

Abstract

In this paper, we present the results of experiments aiming to validate a two-dimensional typology of affective states as a suitable basis for affective classification of texts. Using a corpus of English weblog posts, annotated for mood by their authors, we trained support vector machine binary classifiers to distinguish texts on the basis of their affiliation with one region of the space. We then report on experiments which go a step further, using four-class classifiers based on automated scoring of texts for each dimension of the typology. Our results indicate that it is possible to extend the standard binary sentiment analysis (positive/negative) approach to a two dimensional model (positive/negative; active/passive), and provide some evidence to support a more fine-grained classification along these two axes.

1 Introduction

We are investigating the subjective use of language in text and the automatic classification of texts according to their subjective characteristics, or 'affect'. Our approach is to view affective states (such as 'happy', 'angry') as locations in Osgood's Evaluation-Activation (EA) space (Osgood et al., 1957), and draws on work in psychology which has a long history of work seeking to construct a typology of such affective states (Scherer, 1984). A similar approach has been used more recently to describe emotional states that are expressed in speech (Cowie and Cornelius, 2002; Schröder and Cowie, 2005). Our overall aim is to determine the extent to which such a typology can be validated and applied to the task of text classification using automatic methods. In this paper we describe some initial experiments aimed at validating a basic two dimensional classification of weblog data, first with Support Vector Machine (SVM) binary classifiers, then with Pointwise Mutual Information - Information Retrieval (PMI-IR). The domain of weblog posts is particularly well-suited for this task given its highly subjective nature and the availability of data , including data which has been author-annotated for 'mood', which is a reasonable approximation of 'affect'.

Recent attempts to classify weblog posts have shown modest, but consistent improvements over a 50% baseline, only slightly worse than human performance (Mishne, 2005). One important milestone is the elaboration of a typology of affective states. To devise such a typology, our starting point is Figure 1, which is based on a model of emotion as a multicomponent process (Scherer, 1984). In this model, the distribution of the affective states is the result of analysing similarity judgments by humans for 235 emotion terms[1] using cluster-analysis and multidimensional scaling techniques to map out the structure as a two-dimensional space. The positioning of words is not so much controversial as fuzzy; an affective state such as 'angry' to describe facial expression in speech may have a slightly different location than an 'angry' weblog post. In this model, the well-studied 'sentiment' classification is simply a specific case (left vs. right halves of the space). The experiments we describe here seek to go beyond this basic distinction. They involve an additional dimension of affect, the *activity* dimension, allowing textual data to be classified into four categories corresponding to each of the four quad-

[1] Reduced to less than 100 in Figure 1.

Proceedings of the Workshop on Sentiment and Subjectivity in Text, pages 55–62,
Sydney, July 2006. ©2006 Association for Computational Linguistics

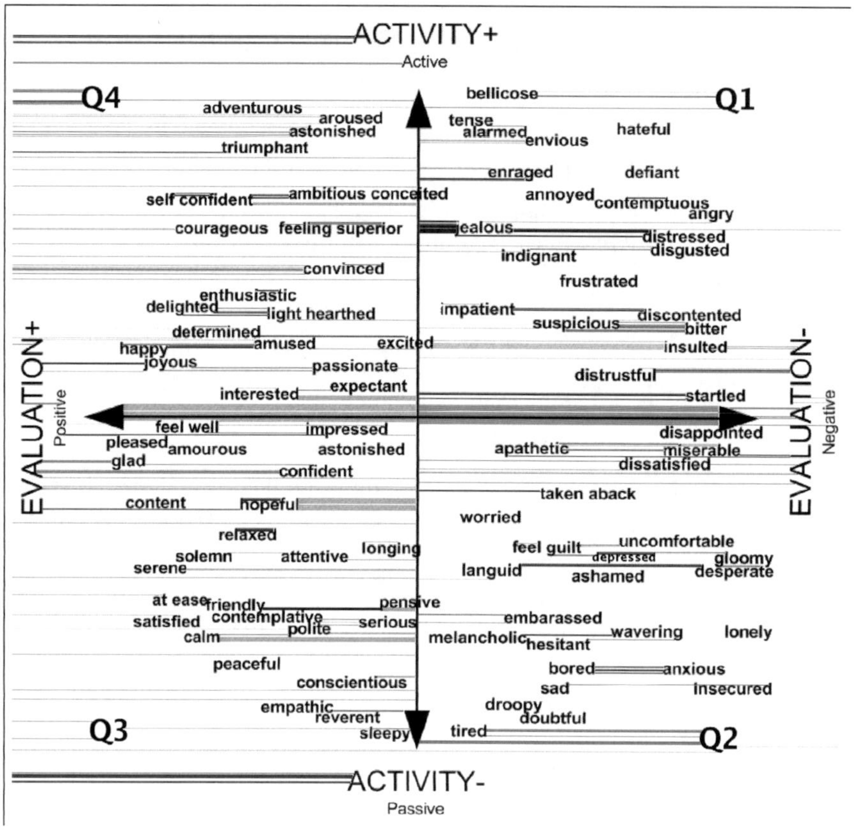

ACTIVITY+
Active
Q4
Q1
bellicose
adventurous
aroused
astonished
triumphant
tense
alarmed
envious
hateful
enraged
defiant
self confident
ambitious
conceited
annoyed
contemptuous
angry
courageous
feeling superior
jealous
distressed
disgusted
indignant
convinced
frustrated
enthusiastic
delighted
light hearthed
impatient
suspicious
discontented
bitter
determined
happy
amused
excited
insulted
joyous
passionate
distrustful
interested
expectant
startled
EVALUATION+
Positive
EVALUATION-
Negative
feel well
impressed
disappointed
pleased
amourous
astonished
apathetic
miserable
glad
confident
dissatisfied
content
hopeful
taken aback
worried
relaxed
solemn
attentive
longing
feel guilt
uncomfortable
depressed
gloomy
serene
languid
ashamed
desperate
at ease
friendly
pensive
satisfied
contemplative
polite
serious
embarassed
calm
melancholic
hesitant
wavering
lonely
peaceful
bored
anxious
conscientious
sad
insecured
empathic
reverent
droopy
doubtful
Q3
sleepy
tired
Q2
ACTIVITY-
Passive

conceited, self confident, courageous, feeling superior, enthusiastic, light hearthed, determined, passionate, expectant, interested, joyous and delighted.

In our experiments, we used 15662 from quadrant Q1 (see Figure 1), 54940 from Q2, 49779 from Q3 and 35634 from Q4.

3 Experiment 1: Distinguishing the four Quadrants

Our hypothesis is that the classification of two disjoint sets of moods should yield a classification accuracy significantly above a baseline of 50%. To verify our hypothesis, we conducted a series of experiments using machine learning to classify weblog posts according to their mood, each class corresponding to one particular quadrant. We used Support Vector Machines (Joachims, 2001) with three basic classic features (unigrams, POS and stems) to classify the posts as belonging to one quadrant or one of the three others. For each classification task, we extracted randomly 1000 testing examples, and trained separately with 2000, 4000, 8000 and 16000 examples. In each case, examples were divided equally among positive and negative examples[3]. The set of features used varied for each of these tasks, they were selected by thresholding each (distinct) training data set, after removing words (unigrams) from the categories poor in affective content (prepositions, determiners, etc.). To qualify as a feature, each unigram, POS or stem had to occur at least three times in the training data. The value of each feature corresponds to its number of occurence in the training examples.

3.1 Results

Our hypothesis is that, if the four quadrants depicted in Figure 1 are a suitable arrangement for affective states in the EA space, a classifier should perform significantly better than chance (50%). Table 1 shows the results for the binary classification of the quadrants. In this table, the first column identifies the classification task in the form 'P vs N', where 'P' stands for positive examples and 'N' for negative examples. The 'Random' row shows results for selecting positive and negative examples randomly from all four quadrants. By micro-averaging accuracy for the classification of each quadrant vs all others (rows 10 to 13), we obtain at least 60% accuracy for the four binary classifications of the quadrants[4]. The first six rows show evidence that each quadrant forms a distinctive whole, as the classifer can easily decide between any two of them.

[3]For instance, 1000 = 500 positives from one QUADRANT + 500 negatives among the other three QUADRANTS.

Testing	Size of training set			
1000 examples	2k	4k	8k	16k
Q1 vs Q3	67%	70%	72%	73%
Q2 vs Q4	61%	64%	65%	67%
Q1 vs Q2	64%	66%	68%	69%
Q2 vs Q3	58%	59%	59%	59%
Q3 vs Q4	59%	60%	60%	61%
Q4 vs Q1	69%	72%	73%	75%
Q1+4 vs Q2+3	56%	58%	58%	61%
Q3+4 vs Q1+2	62%	65%	67%	66%
Random	49%	52%	50%	50%
Q1 vs Q2+3+4	67%	72%	72%	73%
Q2 vs Q1+3+4	59%	60%	63%	63%
Q3 vs Q1+2+4	57%	58%	58%	59%
Q4 vs Q1+2+3	60%	63%	65%	65%
Micro-accuracy	61%	64%	65%	65%

Table 1: Accuracy of binary classification

3.2 Analysis of Results

We introduce now table 2 that shows two thresholds of significance (1% and 5%) for the interpretation of current and coming results. For example, if we have 1000 trials with each trial having a probability of success of 0.5, the likelihood of getting at least 53.7% of the trials right is only 1%. This gives us a baseline to see how significantly well above chance a classifier performs. The SVM algorithm has linearly separated the data for each quadrant according to lexical and POS content (the features). The most sensible explanation is that the features for each class (quadrant) are *semantically* related, a piece of information which is relevant for the model (see section 4). It is safe to conclude that the results cannot be allocated to chance, that there is something else at work that explains the

[4]Micro-averaged accuracy is defined as:

$$\frac{\sum_i (tp_i + tn_i)}{\sum_i (tp_i + tn_i + fp_i + fn_i)}$$

where *tp* stands for "true positive", *fn* for "false negative", etc.

Trials	Prob(Success)	1%	5%
1000	0.50	53.7%	52.6%
750	0.50	54.3%	53.1%
500	0.50	55.2%	53.6%
250	0.50	57.2%	55.2%
1000	0.25	28.2%	27.3%
750	0.25	28.7%	27.6%
500	0.25	29.6%	28.2%
250	0.25	31.6%	29.6%

Table 2: Statistical Significance

accuracies consistently well above a baseline, and this something else is the typology. These results show that the abstraction offered by the four quadrants in the model seems correct. This is also supported by the observation that the classifier shows no improvements over the baseline if trained over a random selection of examples in the entire space.

4 Experiment 2: Classification using Semantic Orientation from Association

Our next goal is to be able to classify a text according to more than four classes (positive/negative, active/passive), by undertaking multi-category classification of texts according to particular regions of the space, (such as 'angry', 'sad', etc.). In order to do that we need a scoring system for each axis. In the following experiments we explore the use of such scores and give some insights into how to transform these scores of affect as measures of affect.

Using binary classifiers, we have already established that if we look at the lexical contents of weblog posts tagged according to their mood by their author, these mood classes tend to cluster according to a two-dimensional typology defined by their semantic orientation: positive or negative (*evaluation*), active or passive (*activity*). Beyond academic importance, the typology really becomes of practical interest if we can classify the posts using pre-defined automated scores for both axis. One strategy of scoring is to extract phrases, including single words, which are good indicators of subjectivity in texts, and score them according to how they relate or 'associate' to one or the other extremity of each axis. This strategy, called Semantic Orientation (SO) from Association (A) has been used successfully (Turney and Littman, 2003) to classify texts or adjectives of all sorts according to their *sentiments* (in our typology this corresponds to the *evaluation* dimension). According to these scores, a text or adjective can be said to have, for example, a more or less positive or negative *evaluation*. We will use this strategy to go further in the validation of our model of affective states by scoring also the *activity* dimension; to our knowledge, this is the first time this strategy is employed to get (text) scores for dimensions other than *evaluation*. In SO-A, we score the strength of the association between an *indicator* from the text and a set of positive or negative words (the paradigms *Pwords* and *Nwords*) capturing the very positive/active or negative/passive semantic orientation of the axis poles. To get the SO-A of a text, we sum over positive scores for indicators positively related to *Pwords* and negatively related to *Nwords* and negative scores for indicators positively related to *Nwords* and negatively related to *Pwords*. In mathematical terms, the SO-A of a text is:

$$\sum_{ind}^{Text}\Big(\sum_{p}^{Pwords} A(ind,p) - \sum_{n}^{Nwords} A(ind,n)\Big)$$

where *ind* stands for indicator. Note that the quantity of *Pwords* must be equal to *Nwords*.

To compute A, (Kamps et al. , 2004) focus on the use of lexical relations defined in WordNet[5] and define a distance measure between two terms which amounts to the length of the shortest path that connects the two terms. This strategy is interesting because it constrains all values to belong to the [-1,+1] range, but can be applied only to a finite set of indicators and has yet to be tested for the classification of texts. (Turney and Littman, 2003) use Pointwise Mutual Information - Information Retrieval (PMI-IR); PMI-IR operates on a wider variety of multi-words indicators, allowing for contextual information to be taken into account, has been tested extensively on different types of texts, and the scoring system can be potentially normalized between [-1,+1], as we will soon see. PMI (Church and Hanks, 1990) between two phrases is defined as:

$$\log_2 \frac{prob(ph_1\ is\ near\ ph_2)}{prob(ph_1) * prob(ph_2)}$$

PMI is positive when two phrases tend to co-occur and negative when they tend to be in a complementary distribution. PMI-IR refers to the fact

[5] `http://wordnet.princeton.edu/.`

that, as in Informtion Retrieval (IR), multiple occurrences in the same document count as just one occurrence: according to (Turney and Littman, 2003), this seems to yield a better measure of semantic similarity, providing some resistance to noise. Computing probabilities using hit counts from IR, this yields to a value for PMI-IR of:

$$\log_n \frac{N * (hits(ph_1\ NEAR\ ph_2) + 1/N)}{(hits(ph_1) + 1) * (hits(ph_2) + 1)}$$

where N is the total number of documents in the corpus. We are going to use this method for computing A in SO-A, which we call SO-PMI-IR. The configuration depicted in the remaining of this section follows mostly (Turney and Littman, 2003).

Smoothing values (1/N and 1) are chosen so that PMI-IR will be zero for words that are not in the corpus, two phrases are considered *NEAR* if they co-occur within a window of 20 words, and $\log_2$ has been replaced by $\log_n$, since the natural log is more common in the literature for log-odds ratio and this makes no difference for the algorithm.

Two crucial aspects of the method are the choice of indicators to be extracted from the text to be classified, as well as the sets of positive and negative words to be used as paradigms for the *evaluation* and *activity* dimensions. The five part-of-speech (POS) patterns from (Turney, 2002) were used for the extraction of indicators, all involving at least one adjective or adverb. POS tags were acquired with TreeTagger (Schmid, 1994)[6]. Ideally, words used as paradigms should be context insensitive, i.e their semantic orientation is either always positive or negative. The adjectives *good, nice, excellent, positive, fortunate, correct, superior* and *bad, nasty, poor, negative, unfortunate, wrong, inferior* were used as near pure representations of positive and negative *evaluation* respectively, while *fast, alive, noisy, young* and *slow, dead, quiet, old* as near pure representations of active and passive *activity* (Summers, 1970).

Departing from (Turney and Littman, 2003), who uses the Alta Vista advanced search with approximately 350 millions web pages, we used the Waterloo corpus[7], with approximately 46 millions pages. To avoid introducing confusing heuristics, we stick to the configuration described above, but (Turney and Littman, 2003) have experimented with different configuation in computing SO-PMI-IR.

[6](Turney and Littman, 2003) uses (Brill, 1994).

[7]`http://canola1.uwaterloo.ca/`.

4.1 The Typology and SO-PMI-IR

We now use the typology with an automated scoring method for semantic orientation. The results are presented in the form of a Confusion Matrix (CM). In this and the following matrices, the top-left cell indicates the overall accuracy[8], the POSitive (ACTive) and NEGative (PASsive) columns represent the instances in a predicted class, the P/T column (where present) indicates the average number of patterns per text (blog post), E/P indicates the average *evaluation* score per pattern and A/P indicates the average *activity* score per pattern. Each row represents the instances in an actual class[9].

First, it is useful to get a clear idea of how the SO-PMI-IR experimental setup we presented compares with (Turney and Littman, 2003) on a human-annotated set of words according to their *evaluation* dimension: the General Inquirer (GI, (Stone, 1966)) lexicon is made of 3596 words (1614 positives and 1982 negatives)[10]. Table 3 summarizes the results. (Turney and Littman, 2003) reports an accuracy of 82.8% while classifying those words, while our experiment yields an accuracy of 76.4% for the same words. Their results show that their classifier errs very slightly towards the negative pole (as shown by the accuracies of both predicted classes) and has a very balanced distribution of the word scores (as shown by the almost equal but opposite in signs values of E/Ps). This is some evidence that the paradigm words are appropriate as near pure representations of positive and negative *evaluation*. By contrast,

(U) 76.4%	POS	NEG	E/P
POS(1614)	59.3%	40.7%	1.5
NEG(1982)	9.6%	90.4%	-4.3
(T) 82.8%	POS	NEG	E/P
POS(1614)	81.2%	18.8%	3.2
NEG(1982)	15.8%	84.2%	-3.6

Table 3: CM for the GI: (U)Us and (T)(Turney and Littman, 2003)

[8]Recall that table 2 gives an interpretation of the statistical signifiance of accuracy, with trials ≈ 750 and Prob(success) = 0.5.

[9]For example, in the comparative evaluation shown in table 3, our classifier classified 59.3% of the 1614 positive instances as positive and 40.7% as negative, with an average score of 1.5 per pattern.

[10]Note that all moods in the typology present in the GI have the same polarity for *evaluation* in both, which is some evidence in favour of the typology.

our classifier appears to be more strongly biased towards the negative pole, probably due to the use of different corpora. This bias[11] should be kept in mind in the interpretation of the results to come.

The second experiment focuses on the words from the typology. Table 4 shows the results. The

81.1%	POS	NEG	P/T	E/P
POS(43)	60.5%	39.5%	1	0.4
NEG(47)	0.0%	100.0%	1	-6.4
66.7%	ACT	PAS	P/T	A/P
ACT(39)	33.3%	66.7%	1	-0.9
PAS(51)	7.8%	92.2%	1	-2.9

Table 4: CM for the Typology affective states

value of 1 under P/T reflects the fact that the experiment amounts, in practical terms, to classifying the annotation of the post (a single word). For the *evaluation* dimension, there is another shift towards the negative pole of the axis, which suggests that words in the typology are distributed not exactly as shown on figure 1, but instead appear to have a true location shifted towards the negative pole. The *activity* dimension also appear to have a negative (i.e passive) bias. There are two main possible reasons for that: words in the typology should be shifted towards the passive pole (as in the *evaluation* case), or the paradigm words for the passive pole are not pure representations of the extremity of the pole [12].

Having established that our classifier has a negative bias for both axes, we now turn to the classification of the quadrants per se. In the next section, we used SO-PMI-IR to classify 1000 randomnly selected blog posts from our corpus, i.e 250 in each of the four quadrants. Some of these posts were found to have no pattern and were therefore not classified, which means that less than 1000 posts were actually classified in each experiment. We also report on the classification of an important subcategory of these moods called the *Big Six* emotions.

[11] Bias can be introduced by the use of a small corpus, inadequate paradigm words or typology. In practice, a quick fix for neutralizing bias would be to normalize the SO-PMI-IR values by subtracting the average. This work aims at tuning the model to remove bias introduced by unsound paradigm words or typology.

[12] At the time of experimenting, we were not aware of an equivalent of the GI to independently verify our paradigm words for activity, but one reviewer pointed out such a resource, see `http://www.wjh.harvard.edu/~inquirer/spreadsheet_guide.htm`.

4.2 Results

Of the 1000 blog posts, there were 938 with at least one pattern. Table 5 shows the accuracy for the classification of these posts.

56.8%	POS	NEG	P/T	E/P
POS(475)	76.2%	23.8%	10	5.2
NEG(463)	63.1%	36.9%	9	3.5
51.8%	ACT	PAS	P/T	A/P
ACT(461)	20.6%	79.4%	8	-4.3
PAS(477)	18.0%	82.0%	11	-4.2

Table 5: CM for all Moods

An important set of emotions found in the literature (Ekman, 1972) has been termed the *Big Six*. These emotions are *fear, anger, happiness, sadness, surprise* and *disgust*. We have used a minimally extended set, adding *love* and *desire* (Cowie and Cornelius, 2002), to cover all four quadrants (we called this set the *Big Eight*). *Fear, anger* and *disgust* belong to quadrant 1, *sadness* and *surprise* (we have taken it to be a synonym of 'taken aback' in the typology) belong to quadrant 2, *love* and *desire* (taken to be synonyms of 'amorous' and 'longing' in the typology) belong to quadrant 3 and *happy* to quadrant 4. Table 6 shows the results for the classification of the blog posts that were tagged with one of these emotions. This amounts to classifying the posts containing only the Big Eight affective states.

59.0%	POS	NEG	P/T	E/P
POS(467)	72.4%	27.6%	9	5.1
NEG(351)	58.7%	41.3%	6	2.3
54.9%	ACT	PAS	P/T	A/P
ACT(357)	23.8%	76.2%	8	-4.4
PAS(461)	21.0%	79.0%	8	-4.6

Table 6: CM for the Big Eight

In the remaining two experiments, blog posts have been classifed using a discrete scoring system. Disregarding the real value of SO, each pattern was scored with a value of +1 for a positive score and -1 for a negative score. This amounts to counting the number of patterns on each side and has the advantage of providing a normalized value for E/T and A/T between -1 and +1. Normalized values are the first step towards a measure of affect, not merely a score, in the sense that it gives an estimate of the strength of affect. We have not classified the posts for which the resulting score was zero, which means that even fewer posts (741) than the previous experiment were actually evaluated. Table 7 shows the results for all moods and table 8 for the Big Eight.

55.7%	POS	NEG	P/T	E/P
POS(374)	53.2%	46.8%	11	0.03
NEG(367)	41.7%	58.3%	9	-0.11
53.3%	ACT	PAS	P/T	A/P
ACT(357)	21.8%	78.2%	8	-0.3
PAS(384)	17.4%	82.6%	12	-0.34

Table 7: CM for all Moods: Discrete scoring

59.8%	POS	NEG	P/T	E/P
POS(373)	52.3%	47.7%	10	0.01
NEG(354)	32.2%	67.8%	9	-0.2
52.8%	ACT	PAS	P/T	A/P
ACT(361)	25.8%	74.2%	10	-0.3
PAS(366)	20.5%	79.5%	9	-0.4

Table 8: CM for the Big Eight: Discrete scoring

4.3 Analysis of Results

Our concerns about the paradigm words for evaluating the *activity* dimension are clearly revealed in the classification results. The classifier shows a heavy negative (passive) bias in all experiments. The overall accuracy for *activity* is consistently below that for *evaluation*: three of them are not statistically significant at 1% (51.8%, 53.3% and 52.8%) and two at even 5% (51.8% and 52.8%). The classifier appears particularly confused in table 5, averaging a score for active posts (-4.3) smaller than for passive posts (-4.2). It is not impossible that the moods present in the typology may have to be shifted towards the passive dimension, but further research should look first at finding better paradigm words for *activity*. A good starting point for the calibration of the classifier for *activity* is the creation of a list of human-annotated words for *activity*, comparable in size to the GI list, combined with an experiment similar to the one for which results are reported in table 3.

With regards to the *evaluation* dimension, tables 5 and 6 reveal a positive bias (despite having a classifier which has a 'built-in' negative bias, see section 4.1). Possible explanations for this phenomenon include the use of irony by people in negative posts, blogs which are expressed in more positive terms than their annotation would suggest, and failure to detect 'negative' contexts for patterns — one example of the latter is provided in table 9. This phenomena appears to be alleviated

Mood:	bored (evaluation-)
Post:	gah!! i need **new music**, any suggestions? by the way, **GOOD MUSIC**.
Patterns:	new music [JJ NN] +4.38 GOOD MUSIC [JJ NN] +53.40
Average SO:	+57.78 (evaluation+)

Table 9: Missclassified post

by the use of discrete scores (see tables 7 and 8). One way of refining the scoring system is to reduce the effect of scoring antonyms as high as synonyms by not counting co-occurences in the corpus where the word 'not' is in the neighbourhood (Turney, 2001). Also,

The long-term goal of this research is to be able to classify texts by locating their normalized scores for *evaluation* and *activity* between -1 and +1, and we have suggested a simple method of achieving that by averaging over discrete scores. However, by combining individual results for *evaluation* and *activity* for each post[13], we can already classify text into one of the four quadrants, and we can expect the average accuracy of this classification to be approximately the product of the accuracy for each dimension. Table 10 shows the results for the classification directly into quadrants of the 727 posts already classified into halves (E±, A±) in table 8. The overall accuracy is 31.1% (expected accuracy is 59.8% * 52.8% = 31.6%). There are biases towards Q2 and Q3, but no clear cases of confusion between two or more classes.

31.1%	Q1	Q2	Q3	Q4
Q1(180)	21.1%	47.8%	22.2%	8.9%
Q2(174)	15.5%	51.1%	25.3%	8.0%
Q3(192)	9.9%	42.2%	40.1%	7.8%
Q4(181)	9.4%	33.7%	44.8%	12.2%

Table 10: CM for Big Eight: Discrete scoring

Finally, our experiments show no correlation between the length of a post (in number of patterns) and the accuracy of the classification.

[13]For example, a post with E- and A+ would be classified in Q1.

5 Conclusion and Future Work

In this paper, we have used a machine learning approach to show that there is a relation between the semantic content of texts and the affective state they (wish to) convey, so that a typology of affective states based on semantic association is a good description of the distribution of affect in a two-dimensional space. Using automated methods to score semantic association, we have demonstrated a method to compute semantic orientation on both dimensions, giving some insights into how to go beyond the customary 'sentiment' analysis. In the classification experiments, accuracies were always above a random baseline, although not always statistically significant. To improve the typology and the accuracies of classifiers based on it, a better calibration of the *activity* axis is the most pressing task. Our next steps are experiments aiming at refining the translation of scores to normalized measures, so that individual affects can be distinguished within a single quadrant. Other interesting avenues are studies investigating how well the typology can be ported to other textual data domains, the inclusion of a 'neutral' tag, and the treatment of texts with multiple affects.

Finally, the domain of weblog posts is attractive because of the easy access to annotated data, but we have found through our experiments that the content is very noisy, annotation is not always consistent among 'bloggers', and therefore classification is difficult. We should not underestimate the positive effects that cleaner data, consistent tagging and access to bigger corpora would have on the accuracy of the classifier.

Acknowledgement

This work was partially funded by the European Commission through the Network of Excellence EPOCH ("Excellence in Processing Open Cultural Heritage"). Thanks to Peter Turney for the provision of access to the Waterloo MultiText System.

References

Eric Brill. 1994. *Some advances in transformation-based part of speech tagging*. Proc. of 12th National Conference on AI. pp. 722-727. Menlo Park, CA: AAAI Press.

Kenneth Ward Church and Patrick Hanks. 1990. *Word association norms, mutual information, and lexicography*. Computational Linguistics. Vol. 16, No 1. pages 22–29, MIT Press, Cambridge, MA, USA.

Roddy Cowie and Randolph R. Cornelius. 2002. *Describing the emotional states that are expressed in speech*. Speech Communication 1228. Elsevier Science B.V.. 20 June 2002, 28 pages.

Paul Ekman. 1972. *Universal and cultural differences in facial expression of emotion*. J.K. Cole (Eds), Nebraska Symposium on Motivation. pp 207-282. Lincoln, University of Nebraska Press.

Thorsten Joachims. 2001. *Learning to Classify Text Using Support Vector Machines*. Kluwer Academic Publishers.

Jaap Kamps and Robert J. Mokken and Maarten Marx and Maarten de Rijke. 2004. *Using WordNet to measure semantic orientation of adjectives*. Proc. of LREC 2004. Vol. IV, pages 1115-1118.

Gilad Mishne. 2005. *Experiments with mood classification in blog posts*. In Style2005 - the 1st Workshop on Stylistic Analysis Of Text For Information Access, at SIGIR 2005.

Charles E. Osgood, George J. Suci, and Percy H. Tannenbaum. 1957. *The Measurement of Meaning*. University of Illinois.

Klaus R. Scherer. 1984. *Emotion as a Multicomponent Process: A model and some cross-cultural data*. In P. Shaver (Ed.) Review of Personality and Social Psych. Vol. 5 (pp. 37-63). Beverley Hills, CA: Sage.

H. Schmid. 1994. *Probabilistic part-of-speech tagging using decision trees*. In International Conf. on New Methods in Language Processing. Manchester UK.

Marc Schröder and Roddy Cowie. 2005. *Towards emotion-sensitive multimodal interfaces*. Invitated talk at the Workshop on "Adapting the interaction style to affective factors" pp. 235-253. User Modelling 2005, July 25, Edinburgh.

Philip J. Stone and Dexter C. Dunphy and Marshall S. Smith and Daniel M. Ogilvie. 1966. *The General Inquirer: A Computer Approach to Content Analysis*. MIT Press. `http://www.webuse.umd.edu:9090/`.

Gene F. Summers. 1970. *Attitude measurement*. Chicago: Rand McNally. pp. 235-253.

Peter Turney. 2001. *Mining the Web for Synonyms: PMI-IR versus LSA on TOEFL*. European Conference on Machine Learning. pp 491–502. `citeseer.nj.nec.com/turney01mining.html`.

Peter D. Turney. 2002. *Thumbs Up or Thumbs Down? Semantic Orientation Applied to Unsupervised Classification of Reviews*. Proc. of the ACL 2002. Philadelphia, USA. July 8-10, 2002, pp 417-424.

Peter D. Turney and Michael L. Littman. 2003. *Measuring praise and criticism: Inference of semantic orientation from association*. ACM Trans. Inf. Syst. 21(4):315346.

Author Index

Barnden, John A., 47

Cardie, Claire, 9
Carter, Richard, 23
Chinchor, Nancy, 23

Dinesh, Nikhil, 31

Evans, Roger, 55

Fujii, Atsushi, 15
Furuse, Osamu, 39

Généreux, Michel, 55
Gregory, Michelle L., 23

Hendley, Robert J., 47
Hetzler, Elizabeth, 23
Hiroshima, Nobuaki, 39
Hovy, Eduard, 1

Ishikawa, Tetsuya, 15

Joshi, Aravind, 31

Kataoka, Ryoji, 39
Kim, Soo-Min, 1

Lee, Alan, 31

Prasad, Rashmi, 31

Stoyanov, Veselin, 9

Turner, Alan, 23

Wallington, Alan M., 47
Webber, Bonnie, 31
Whitney, Paul, 23

Yamada, Setsuo, 39

Zhang, Li, 47

Association for Computational Linguistics
209 N. Eighth Street
Stroudsburg, Pennsylvania 18360